THE LAW OF WILLS

Albert Keating
B.C.L., LL.B., LL.M, B.L.

DUBLIN
ROUND HALL SWEET AND MAXWELL
2002

Published in 2002 by

Round Hall Ltd.
43 Fitzwilliam Place
Dublin 2
Ireland

Typeset by
Devlin Typesetting, Dublin

Printed by
Colour Books, Dublin

A CIP catalogue record for this book is available
from the British Library

ISBN 1-85800-302-4

Preface

While the title of the book is *The Law of Wills*, it covers all the areas also associated with succession law. It was thought preferable to give it the title of *The Law of Wills* rather than *Succession Law* in order to emphasise that academic knowledge alone of this subject does not present the complete picture of an area that is dealt with by almost every firm in the country on a regular basis. It might seem morbid to say so but it is an area that stands astride the living and the dead. A person goes to make his will in the belief that it will encapsulate his wishes to take effect on his death. It is the testator with his own special wishes who will bring the rules to life and it will be his death that will give effect to those wishes. The rules and the will to which they give life are therefore inseparable. The will will come to life on the death of the testator and it is at this point that the personal representatives become involved. Before they can carry out the wishes of the testator, they must first obtain probate, and, again, it is observed that an academic knowledge of the rules alone will not reflect the true practical nature of the subject. Therefore, the aim of the book is to give parity of treatment to the academic and to the practical.

As a law lecturer, I have a certain understanding of the needs of students. While they may eventually go on to become prosperous practitioners and afford the luxury of the professional books in the field, as students, however, they may have lean years, and a textbook with a less expensive price tag may be more in keeping with their pockets; they may have to content themselves for the time being with viewing the professional texts as points of reference rather than as purchases. Monetary considerations should not, however, be the sole criterion for producing a text; regard must be had to the sufficiency of the material covered by it. While I accept the responsibility for the material provided by this book, I also enjoin the student to listen to his or her lecturer and to refer to the more substantial texts on the subject when reading this essential text.

I would like also like to thank my publishers Round Hall Sweet and Maxwell, in particular Catherine Dolan, Teresa Dowling, Dave Ellis and Orla Fee for their commitment to this book.

Albert Keating
June 2002
College Street Campus
Waterford Institute of Technology

Table of Contents

Preface v
Abbreviations xi
Table of Cases xv
Table of Statutes xix
Table of Rules... xxii

1. **Anatomy of a Will**
   Instructions for Making a Will 1
   Form 1
   Due Execution 2
   Capacity..2
   Probate..2
   Letters of Administration with the Will 3
   Letters of Administration Intestate..3
   Letters of Administration *De Bonis Non*...3
   Caveats and Citations 4

2. **The Due Execution of a Will**
   Definition of a Will 5
   The Testator's Signature..5
   The Testator Directing Another to Sign on His Behalf..........................6
   The Testator Acknowledging His Signature 6
   The Position of the Testator's Signature 6
   The Signing by the Witnesses 7
   The Witnesses' Signatures 8
   The Position of the Witnesses' Signatures...8
   Presumption of Due Execution 9
   The Principle of Knowledge and Approval...10
   Alterations 12
   Incorporation of Documents..13
   Codicils...14
   The Liability of a Solicitor 14
   A Will is Effective on Death Only 14

3. **Capacity to Make a Will, Undue Influence and Fraud**
   Capacity..17
   Age of the Testator 17

Sound Disposing Mind 18
Mental Ill-Health 19
Undue Influence 21
Fraud 21

4. **The Revocation and Revival of Wills**
Revocation.. 23
Methods of Revocation 23
Revocation by Subsequent Marriage.. 23
A Will Made in Contemplation of Marriage 24
Revocation by Destruction 24
The Act of Destruction... 25
The Intention to Revoke 25
By Inference 26
By Presumption 26
Revocation by Testamentary Instrument 27
Revocation Resulting in Intestacy.. 28
Revocation by Codicil 28
The Doctrine of Dependent Relative Revocation............................ 28
Revival of Wills... 29
Revival by Re-Execution.. 29
Revival by Codicil... 30

5. **Testamentary Gifts, Statutory Rights and Claims**
Testamentary Gifts.. 31
Classification of Testamentary Gifts 31
Failure of Testamentary Gifts.. 33
Income 35
Interest 35
Inheritance Tax 36
Statutory Rights and Claims.. 39
The Amount of the Legal Right Share 39
The Nature of the Legal Right... 40
Renunciation of the Legal Right 42
The Right of Election 42
The Extinguishment of the Legal Right 44
Provision for Children 44
The Moral Duty of a Testator 45
Proper Provision 46
The Court Order 47
Time for Making an Application.. 48
Disinheriting Dispositions Made by the Deceased.......................... 48
Loss of Succession Rights.. 48

6. The Rules of Intestacy
An Intestate 51
Succession Act Rules of Intestacy 52
Intestate Share of Surviving Spouse...52
Intestate Share of Children...53
The Principle of Advancement 53
Intestate Share of Parents 55
Intestate Share of Brothers and Sisters.....................................56
Intestate Share of Nephews and Nieces 56
Intestate Share of Next-of-Kin 57
Tracing Next-of-Kin...58
Partial Intestacy 58
The State as Ultimate Intestate Successor.................................59
The Effect of Disclaiming an Intestate Share............................59
Loss of Intestate Succession Rights 59

7. The Personal Representatives
Executors and Administrators 61
Executors...61
Renunciation by an Executor 63
Administrators...63
Devolution of the Estate..64
The Duties of Personal Representatives.....................................65
The Power of Personal Representatives to
    Appropriate the Deceased's Estate 66
The Liability of Personal Representatives 67

8. Probate Jurisdiction
Non-Contentious Jurisdiction..69
The Probate Office 69
District Probate Registry 69
Contentious Jurisdiction..70
The Nature of the Grant 71
The Probate of a Will 71

9. A Grant of Probate
Entitlement to Apply for a Grant...73
The Necessary Documentation...73
The Original Will 73
The Oath of Executor 74
The Death Certificate 76
The Inland Revenue Affidavit...77
Probate Tax..77
A De Bonis Non Grant..78

10. A Grant of Letters of Administration with the Will
The Nature of the Grant 79
Persons Entitled to Apply for a Grant 79
The Necessary Documentation 80
The Administrator's Oath 81
The Administration Bond 81
A *De Bonis Non* Grant with the Will Annexed 81

11. A Grant of Letters of Administration Intestate
Persons Entitled to Apply for a Grant 83
The Necessary Documentation 86
A *De Bonis Non* Grant Intestate 86

12. Caveats and Citations
Caveats 87
Citations 89

Appendices
Appendix 1 - Specimen Instruction Sheet 93
Appendix 2 - Specimen Wills 95
Appendix 3 - Probate Forms 101
Appendix 4 - Succession Act Forms 115

Index 121

Abbreviations

Ad. & E.	Adolphus & Ellis's Reports (1834–1841)
Add.	Addams' Ecclesiastical Reports (1822–1826)
All E.R.	All England Law Reports
A.C./App. Cas.	Appeal Cases (A.C. – 1891 to date)
Atk.	Atkyns (1736–1755)
B. & A.	Barnewell & Adolphus' King's Bench Reports (1830–1834)
B. & Ald.	Barnewall & Alderson (1817–1822)
B. & S.	Best & Smith (1861–1870)
Beav.	Beavan's Rolls Court Reports (1838–1866)
Bing.	Bingham's Common Pleas Reports (1822–1840)
Bro. Ch. C.	Brown's Chancery Cases (1778–1794)
Carth.	Carthew's King's Bench Reports (1668–1701)
C.B.N.S.	Common Bench Reports (New Series) (1856–1865)
Ch./Ch. D.	Chancery (1891 to date) (1875–1890)
Ch. App.	Chancery Appeals (1865–1875)
Cl. & F.	Clark & Finnelly's House of Lords Cases (1831–1846)
C.L.Y.B.	Current Law Year Book
Co./Co. Rep.	Coke's King's Bench Reports (Eliz. I–James I)
Cox Eq.	Cox's Equity Cases (1745–1797)
Cowp.	Cowper's King's Bench Reports (1774–1778)
Cr.M. & R.	Crompton, Meeson & Roscoe's Exchequer Reports (1834–1835)
Cr. & M.	Crompton & Meeson's Exchequer Reports (1832–1834)
Cr. & Ph.	Craig & Phillips' Chancery Reports (1840–1841)
Curt.	Curteis' Ecclesiastical Reports (1834–1844)
D. & War.	Drury & Warren's Irish Chancery Reports (1841–1843)
Dea. & Sw.	Deane & Swabey's Ecclesiastical Reports (1855–1857)
De G. & J.	De Gex & Jones' Chancery Reports (1856–1859)
De G. & Sm.	De Gex & Smale's Vice-Chancellor's Reports (1846–1852)
De G.F. & J.	De Gex, Fisher & Jones' Chancery Reports (1831–1846)
De G.J. & S.	De Gex, Jones & Smith's Chancery Reports

	(1831–1846)
De G.M. & G.	De Gex, Macnaghten & Gordon's Chancery Reports (1851–1857)
Dick.	Dicken's Chancery Reports (1559–1792)
Dr. & Sm.	Drewry & Smale's Vice Chancellor's Reports (1859–1865)
Dr. & War.	Drury & Warren's Irish Chancery Reports (1841–1843)
Drew.	Drewry's Vice Chancellor's Reports (1852–1859)
E. & B.	Ellis & Blackburn's Queen's Bench Reports (1852–1858)
E. & E.	Ellis & Ellis' Queen's Bench Reports (1858–1861)
Eq.	Equity Cases (1866–1875)
Esp. N.P.	Espinasse's Nisi Prius Reports (1793–1810)
Fam.	Family Division (1972 to date)
Fam. L.J.	Family Law Journal
H. & C.	Hurlstone & Coltman (1862–1866)
Hag. Ecc.	Haggard's Ecclesiastical Reports (1827–1833)
Hare	Hare's Chancery Reports (1841–1853)
H.L.C./H.L. Cas.	House of Lords Cases (1847–1866)
Hurl. & C.	Hurlstone & Coltman's Exchequer Reports (1862–1866)
I.C.L.M.D.	Irish Current Law Monthly Digest
I.L.T.	Irish Law Times
Ir. Eq.	Irish Equity Reports (1838–1850)
Ir. Jur. Rep.	Irish Jurist Reports (1935 to date)
Ir. R. C.L.	Irish Reports, Common Law
I.L.R.M.	Irish Law Reports Monthly
I.L.T.R.	Irish Law Times Reports
I.R.	Irish Reports (1833–1893) (1893 with date to date)
John. & H.	Johnson & Hemming's Vice-Chancellor's Reports (1859–1862)
Jur.	Jurist (1837–1854)
K. & J.	Kay & Johnson's Vice Chancellor's Reports (1854–1958)
K.B.	King's Bench Division (1901–1952)
Keen	Keen's Rolls Court Reports (1836–1838)
Lee	Lee's Ecclesiastical Judgements (1752–1758)
L.J.C.P.	Law Journal Reports, New Series, Common Pleas
L.J. Ch.	Law Journal Reports, Chancery (1831–1946)
L.J.Ir.	Law Journal, Irish
L.J.P.D. & A.	Law Journal Reports, New Series, Probate, Divorce, Admiralty (1876–1946)
L.J.P.M. & A.	Law Journal Reports, Probate, Matrimonial &

	Admiralty (1860–1865)
L.J.P. & M.	Law Journal Reports, New Series, Probate & Matrimonial (1858–1875)
L.R. H.L.	Law Reports, House of Lords (1866–1875)
L.R. Ir.	Law Reports, Ireland (1878–1893)
L.R.P. & D.	Law Reports, Probate & Divorce Cases (1865–1875)
L.T./L.T.R.	Law Times Reports (1859–1947)
Lutw.	Lutwyche's Common Pleas Reports
M. & Gr.	Manning & Granger (1840–1844)
M. & K.	Mylne & Keen (1832–1835)
M. & W.	Meeson & Welsby's Exchequer Reports (1836–1847)
Mac. & G.	Macnaghten & Gordon's Chancery Reports (1849–1852)
Madd.	Maddock's Reports (1815–1822)
McCl. & Y.	McCleland & Younge's Exchequer Reports (1824–1825)
Mer.	Merivale's Chancery Reports (1815–1817)
Milw.	Milward's Irish Ecclesiastical Reports
Mod. Rep.	Modern Reports (1669–1732)
Moo. P.C./Moore P.C.	Moore's Privy Council Cases (1836–1862)
My. & Cr.	Mylne & Craig's Chancery Reports (1835–1841)
N.C.	Notes of Cases (1841–1850)
N.I.	Northern Ireland Law Reports (1925 to date)
N.I.Y.B.	Northern Ireland Year Book
N.Z.L.R.	New Zealand Law Reports (1883 to date)
O.R.	Ontario Reports (1823 to date)
P.	Law Reports, Probate (1890 to date)
P. & D.	Law Reports, Probate & Divorce (1865–1875)
P. & M.	Probate & Matrimonial (1858–1875)
P.D.	Law Reports, Probate, Divorce and Admiralty Division (1875–1890)
P. Wms.	Peere Williams' Chancery Reports (1695–1735)
Ph.	Phillips' Chancery Reports
Phill. Ecc. Judg.	Phillimore's Ecclesiastical Judgments (1809–1821)
Phill. Ecc. R.	Phillimore's Ecclesiastical Reports (1809–1821)
Prec. Ch.	Precedents in Chancery (1689–1722)
Q.B./Q.B.D.	Queen's Bench Division (1841 to date) (1875–1890)
Rob./Rob. Eccl.	Robertson's Ecclesiastical Reports (1844–1853)
Rus.	Russell's Chancery Reports (1823–1829)
Russ. & M.	Russell & Mylne's Chancery Reports (1829–1833)
Salk.	Salkeld's King's Bench Reports (1689–1712)

Sch. & Lef.	Schoales & Lefroy (1802–1807)
Sim.	Simons' Vice Chancellor's Reports (1826–1852)
S.J.	Solicitors' Journal (1857 to date)
Sw. & Tr.	Swabey & Tristram's Ecclesiastical Reports (1858–1865)
Taunt.	Taunton's Common Pleas Reports (1807–1819)
T.L.R.	Times Law Reports (1884–1950) (1951 to date)
Turn. & R.	Turner & Russell's Chancery Reports (1822–1825)
Vern.	Vernon's Chancery Reports (1681–1719)
Ves. Jun.	Vesey Junior's Chancery Reports (1754–1817)
Ves. Sen.	Vesey Senior's Chancery Reports (1746–1755)
Wightw.	Wightwick's Exchequer Reports (1810–1811)
W.L.R.	Weekly Law Reports (1953 to date)
W.N.	Weekly Notes (1866–1952)
Y. & C.	Younge & Collyer's Exchequer Reports (1834–1842)
You.	Younge's Exchequer Reports (1830–1832)

Table of Cases

Adams v. Lavander M'Cl. & Y 41 5-10
Bell v. Fothergill L.R. 2 P. 148 4-06
Benn, In the Goods of [1938] I.R. 313 2-11
Bennett v. Brumfitt L.R. 3 C.P. 28 2-02
Blackhall, In the Estate of, unreported, Supreme Court, April 1, 1998 2-10
Boughton v. Knight L.R. 3 P. & D. 64 3-03
Bowlby, Re [1904] 2 Ch. 685 5-10
Bulloch, In the Estate of [1968] N.I. 96 2-07
C. and F. v. W.C. and T.C. [1989] I.L.R.M. 815 5-27
Cassidy, In the Goods of [1904] 2 I.R. 427 7-04
Casson v. Dade 1 Bro. Ch. C. 98 2-06
Cheese v. Lovejoy 2 P.D. 251 4-05
Clifford, Re [1912] 1 Ch. 29 5-05
Countess of Durham, In the Goods of 3 Curt. 57 2-12
Cummins, Re the Estate of: O'Dwyer v. Keegan [1997]
    2 I.L.R.M. 401 .... 5-20, 5-21
Darby, In the Goods of 4 N.C. 427 2-12
Day's W.T., Re [1962] 1 W.L.R. 1419 5-09
Duffy v. Kearney and Duffy, unreported, High Court, O'Hanlon J.
    August 10, 1994 3-04
Dunne v. Heffernan, unreported, Supreme Court,
    November 26, 1997 7-10
E.B. v. S.S. [1998] 2 I.L.R.M. 141 5-27
Early, In the Estate of [1980] I.R. 223 2-09
Emerson, In the Goods of 9 L.R. Ir. 443 2-02
Eyre, In the Goods of [1905] 2 I.R. 540 4-11
Fulton v. Kee [1961] N.I. 1 2-03
G.M., Re: F.M. v. T.A.M. 106 I.L.T.R. 82 .... 5-27, 5-28
Garner, In the Goods of 1 L.R. Ir. 507 2-07
Gillet v. Rogers 108 L.T. 732 3-03
Glynn, Deceased, In the Goods of: Glynn v. Glynn [1990]
    2 I.R. 326 .... 2-10, 3-04
Gray, In the Estate of [1963] 107 S.J. 156 4-04
Gunning, Re [1918] 1 I.R. 221 7-10
H. v. H. [1978] I.R. 138 7-09
H. v. O. [1978] I.R. 194 7-09
Hall v. Hall L.R. 1 P. & D. 481 3-05
Harrison v. Harrison 8 Ves. 185 2-07

Harrison, Re 30 Ch.D. 390 5-08
Healy v. Mac Gillycuddy and Lyons [1978] I.L.R.M. 175 3-05
Hine, In the Goods of [1893] P. 282 4-07
Hudson v. Parker 1 Rob. 14 2-04
Irvine, In the Goods of [1919] 2 I.R. 485 4-15
J. de B. v. H.E. de B. [1991] 2 I.R. 105 5-26
J.H., Deceased, In the Goods of [1984] I.R. 599 .... 5-26, 5-28
Jones [1976] Ch. 200 4-07
Kavanagh, Re; Healy v MacGillycuddy and Lyons [1978]
    I.L.R.M. 175 3-05
Kavanagh v. Fegan [1932] I.R. 566 2-04
Kieran, In the Goods of [1933] I.R. 222 2-02
L. v. L., [1978] I.R. 288 5-28
Lemming, Re [1912] 1 Ch. 665 5-05
Madden, In the Goods of [1905] 2 I.R. 612 2-05
Maddoch, In the Goods of L.R. 3 P. & D. 169 2-07
Margarry v. Robinson 12 P.D. 8 4-06
McDonald v. Norris [1999] I.L.R.M. 270 5-25
McElroy v. Flynn and O'Flynn [1991] I.L.R.M. 294 6-13
Millar, In the Goods of [1931] I.R. 364 4-13
Mulhall v. Mulhall [1936] I.R. 712 2-06
Newton v. Clarke 2 Curt. 320 2-06
Newton v. Newton 7 Ir. Jur. (n.s.) 129 2-12
O'Donnell v. O'Donnell, unreported, High Court, Kelly J.,
    March 24, 1999 3-04
Paget, In the Goods of 47 I.L.T.R. 284 4-09
Parker v. Felgate 8 P.D. 171 3-03
Pearce, Re [1909] 1 Ch. 819 5-09
Pearse, Re the Goods of L.R. 1 P. 382 2-12
Perera v. Perera [1901] A.C. 354 3-03
Pilot v. Gainfort [1931] P. 103 4-04
Pollock, Re [1943] Ch. 338 5-10
Rattenbury, Re [1906] 1 Ch. 667 5-10
Reilly v. McEntee [1984] I.L.R.M. 572 .... 5-21, 5-23
Ross v. Caunters [1980] Ch. 297 2-14
Sallis v. Jones [1935] P. 43 4-04
Stamford v. White [1901] P. 46 4-07
Steven, Re s [1899] 1 Ch. 162 7-10
Stoodley, Re [1916] 1 Ch. 242 4-14
Tankard, Re [1942] Ch. 69 7-10
Taudy, In the Goods of 27 L.R. Ir. 114 7-02
Urquhart, Re [1974] I.R. 197 .... 5-20, 5-21, 5-23
Wall v. Hegarty and Callanan [1980] I.L.R.M. 124 2-14
West v. West (1921) [1921] 2 I.R. 34 4-15

West, Re [1909] 2 Ch. 180 5-09
White, In the Goods of 3 L.R. Ir. 413..4-06, 4-08
Wilmot, In the Goods of 1 Sw. & Tr. 36 2-12
Wingrove v. Wingrove 11 P.D. 81 3-05
Woodroofe v. Creed [1894] 1 I.R. 508 2-12
Woodroofe, Re [1953-1954] Ir. Jur. Rep. 36 7-02

Table of Statutes

Adoption Acts 1952-1988 11-01
Capital Acquisitions Tax Act 1976 5-11
    s.38 9-14
    Second Sched., Pt. I, para. 9 5-16
Conveyancing Act 1881 ....App. 2
Conveyancing Act 1911 ....App. 2
Family Law (Divorce) Act 1996
    s.46 5-30
Family Law (Miscellaneous Provisions) Act 1997 6-16
    s.6 6-16
    s.73 6-16
Finance Act 1894 9-14
Finance Act 1993 9-17
Finance Act 2000
    s.151 5-16
Finance Act 2001
    s.225 9-17
    s.272 5-14
Legitimacy Act 1931 6-08
    s.9 11-02
Marriages Act 1972 3-02
    s.1(1) 3-02
Registration of Title Act 1964
    s.61 .... 7-08, App. 4
Settled Land Acts 1882-1890 ....App. 2
Status of Children Act 1987 .... 5-25, 5-32, 6-04, 6-05, 6-08, 6-09, 11-02
    s.27(3) 11-01
Succession Act 1965 .... 1-03, 1-07, 2-01, 5-03, 5-18, 5-23, 6-02, 6-04, 6-08
    .... 7-06, 7-05, 9-03, 9-12, 11-01, 11-02, 11-03
    s.3 6-01
    s.3(1) 5-02, 5-03
    s.4 5-03
    s.4(a) 5-03
    s.10(1) 7-05
    s.10(2) 7-05
    s.10(3) 7-05
    s.10(4) 7-05
    s.10(4)(a) 7-05

s.12(1) 7-05
s.12(3) 7-05
s.13 .... 6-01, 7-01
s.14 5-03
s.23(1) 7-02
s.23(1)(a) 7-02
s.23(1)(b) 7-02
s.34 10-05
s.34(3) 5-17
s.45(1) 7-06
s.50(1) 7-07
s.50(1)(a) 7-07
s.52(2) 7-08
s.53 .... App. 4
s.53(1) 7-08
s.54(2) 7-08
s.55 .... 7-09, App. 2, App. 4
s.55(3) 7-09
s.56 .... 5-12, 7-09, 8-04, 9-16, App. 4
s.56(5)(a) 7-09
s.57 .... App. 2, App. 4
s.63 .... 6-05, 6-07, App. 2
s.63(4) 6-05
s.66 6-02
s.67(1) 6-03
s.67(2) 6-03
s.67(2)(a) 6-03
s.67(2)(b) 6-03
s.67(3) 6-04
s.67(4) 6-03, 6-04
s.68 6-08
s.69(1) 6-10
s.70(1) 6-11
s.70(2) 6-11
s.71(1) 6-12
s.71(2) 6-12
s.72 A 6-16
s.73 .... 6-15, 6-16
s.74 6-14
s.77 .... 3-01, 3-02, 3-03
s.77(1) 2-10
s.78 .... 2-01, 2-02, 2-03, 2-06, 2-13, 3-01
    r.1 2-05
    r.2 2-04

r.3 2-05
r.4 2-05
r.5 2-05
s.82 5-07
s.85 4-02
s.85(1) 4-04
s.85(2) 4-06, 4-14
s.86 2-11
s.87 .... 4-16, 4-17
s.92 5-03
s.98 5-06
s.99 5-08
s.109(1) 5-19
s.109(2) 5-19
s.111 .... 5-19, 5-20, 5-21, App. 4
s.111(1) 5-19
s.111(2) 5-19
s.112 5-19
s.113 .... 5-20, 5-22
s.115 .... 5-21, 5-23, 8-04, App. 4
s.115(4) 5-23
s.117 .... 5-12, 5-25, 5-27, 5-28, 5-29, 5-32, 6-17, 8-04
s.117(1) 5-25, 5-27, 5-28
s.117(2) 5-28
s.117(6) 5-30
s.120(1) 6-17
s.120(5) 6-17
s.121 .... 5-31, 8-04
Pt. VI 6-02
Pt. IX .... 5-19, 9-16, App. 4
Pt. X 6-03
Wills Act 1837
s.7 3-02

Table of Rules

Land Registration Rules 1972 ....App. 4
Rules of the Superior Courts 1962 7-04
Rules of the Superior Courts 1986 .... 7-04, 10-01, 10-04
    Order 79 ....8-05, 10-02
        r.1.. 10-02
        r.2.. 10-02
        r.3.. 10-02
        r.4.. 10-02
        r.5.. 7-04, 8-05, 10-02, 11-04, 11-05
        r.5(1).. 11-01, 11-03
        r.5(1)(c) 11-02
        r.5(2)... 11-01
        r.5(3)... 11-01
        r.5(4)... 11-01
        r.5(5)... 11-01
        r.5(6)..9-19, 10-06
        r.5(7)... 10-02
        r.5(9)(a) 10-02
        r.10... 2-11
        rr.41-51 12-02
        rr.52-58 12-04
        r.62... 2-10
    Pt. II... 10-05

Chapter 1

Anatomy of a Will

Instructions for Making a Will

1-01 The first step towards the making of a will is the completion of an instruction sheet prepared by the testator's solicitor. This is a form of questionnaire which helps to ascertain the extent of the testator's property and the way in which he wishes to dispose of it by his will. The preparation of the will shall be structured on the testator's wishes expressed in the instruction sheet. This will also be the point at which professional advice will be given in relation to the statutory rights and claims of the testator's spouse and children, if any, and also the liability of the testator's beneficiaries to pay inheritance tax, if any. The names and addresses of the executors will also be recorded in the instruction sheet. A specimen instruction sheet is provided in Appendix 1.

Form

1-02 While a will must be prepared in accordance with the testator's instructions, its form, however, may be shaped by such factors as his marital status and the existence of dependent children at the time the will is made. The testator, for instance, may be a married man (or woman) who wishes not only to provide for his wife (or husband) but also for his children, and, because of their age, trustees may have to be appointed to look after their interests (see Appendix 2, Specimen Wills Nos. 1 and 2), or the testator may be unmarried and may wish to benefit near relatives, perhaps nephews and nieces (see Appendix 2, Specimen Will No. 3). However, regardless of form, all wills share certain basic features. A will normally commences with the testator's name and address followed by a revocation clause revoking all former wills (if any) (see Chapter 4). It will then go on to appoint the executors named by the testator in the instruction sheet who may also be required to double as trustees in the event of there being children under the age of majority (*i.e.* under 18 years). The executors will then be directed to discharge the testator's funeral and testamentary expenses and any debts owing and due by him. This will be followed by the gifts of the testator's property or "estate" (see Chapter 5). Where a gift consists of money or personal property *i.e.* personal estate, it is known as a legacy or bequest; if it is one of land or a house *i.e.* real estate, it is known as a devise (see Chapter 5). The gifts of specified personal estate and real estate may then be followed by a gift of the remainder of the testator's real and personal estate and such will be a gift of the "residuary" real and personal estate. The latter type of gift will include all of the testator's estate which was not disposed of in the earlier parts of the will and will also include property acquired by him between the making of the will and his death (see Chapter 5). In the absence of a gift of the residue of his estate, property undisposed of by his will, will be distributed in accordance with the rules of intestacy, *i.e.* a partial intestacy (see Chapter 6).

Due Execution

1-03 The date of the will appears next. This is followed by a space allowed for the testator's signature. Below that space an attestation clause appears: such a clause simply reiterates that the provisions of the Succession Act 1965 regarding the "due execution" of a will have been satisfied, *i.e.* the testator signed in the joint presence of two witnesses (see Chapter 2). However, before the testator signs his name, the will should first be read over to him by his solicitor or it may be read by himself to satisfy another legal principle that he knew and approved of the contents of his will (see Chapter 2).

Capacity

1-04 A testator must be at least 18 years of age to have legal capacity to make a will and also be of "sound disposing mind" (see Chapter 3). There is no ceiling limit as regards the age of a testator; thus, a person may make a will at any age over 18. However, as a will may be challenged on the grounds of lack of capacity of the testator, a medical certificate may be required in the case of an elderly testator, particularly so where old age is accompanied by illness, verifying that he has sufficient capacity to make a will. It may also be noted here that pressure exerted on a testator to make a will benefiting the person exerting the pressure may amount to "undue influence" and may nullify the will.

Probate

1-05 Although a will takes effect or "speaks" from the date of death, the executors are not automatically entitled to administer and distribute the testator's estate from that date until they apply for and obtain a grant of probate (see Chapter 9). When applying for a grant of probate, all the necessary documentation must first be prepared and lodged in either the probate office or a district probate registry (see Chapters 8 and 9). Once a grant of probate is obtained, the executors may then proceed with the administration and distribution of the deceased testator's estate.

Letters of Administration with the Will

1-06 It may happen, however, that the executors appointed by the will have predeceased the testator or that they may wish to renounce their office of executor, and if such is the case, a grant of probate cannot be applied for but instead an application may be made for a grant of letters of administration with the will annexed by the person entitled to apply for such a grant (see Chapter 10). There is a certain order of priority of persons who are entitled to apply for such a grant and the person first entitled, if he is willing to apply for such a grant, must first prepare the necessary documentation for such a grant (see Chapter 10).

Letters of Administration Intestate

1-07 Even though a will is made, it may be deemed invalid because of its failure to satisfy the statutory provisions regarding due execution or it may be ineffective because of the predecease of the beneficiaries. In such a case an intestacy will ensue and it will be the same as if the testator had made no will at all. In the case of an intestacy, an administrator will be appointed in accordance with the order of priority of persons entitled to apply for a grant of letters of administration intestate (see Chapter 11), and, once a grant is made, the administrator will then proceed to distribute the estate among those entitled under the rules of intestacy in the Succession Act 1965 (see Chapter 6). The application for such a grant must be accompanied by the necessary documentation (see Chapter 11).

Letters of Administration *De Bonis Non*

1-08 A grant *de bonis non* must be applied for where an executor or administrator dies or becomes incapacitated during the course of administering an estate; but before a new administrator can be appointed to continue with the administration, the necessary documentation must first be lodged and the type of grant which will then issue is known as a *de bonis non* grant (see Chapters 9, 10 and 11). The person next entitled in accordance with the order of priority after the death of the executor or administrator will be entitled to apply for such a grant (see Chapters 9, 10 and 11).

Caveats and Citations

1-09 A person with an interest in the estate of the deceased testator may wish to be informed when a grant of probate is applied for by the executors. Such a person may, for instance, be a member of the testator's family who has been excluded from the will and may wish to challenge its validity. A caveat may be used for this purpose and once lodged in the probate office he will thereafter be informed of any application for a grant of probate (see Chapter 12). It may happen that the executors are slow in applying for a grant of probate, and if such is the case, any beneficiary who is dissatisfied with the progress of the application may have a citation issued from the probate office requiring the executors to apply for a grant or else the beneficiary himself may apply for a grant (see Chapter 12).

CHAPTER 2

The Due Execution of a Will

Definition of a Will

2-01 A will consists of the testamentary wishes of the testator expressed in writing and duly executed in accordance with the statutory rules to take effect on death. The main body of legislation dealing with the making of wills is the Succession Act 1965. Section 78 of the Act commences by providing that a will, in order to be valid, must be in writing and goes on to provide that for a will to be duly executed, it must be signed or acknowledged in the presence of two witnesses.

The Testator's Signature

2-02 While section 78 of the 1965 Act provides that a will must be signed, it is silent, however, on the question of what constitutes a sufficient signature. It is obvious that the section envisages a testator signing his signature in the usual way; but will his signature be sufficient if he does not make his signature in the accustomed way, or, indeed, what will constitute a signing if he happens to be illiterate? One may find a testator who has adopted a swift way of signing documents in the course of business, or out of affectation, by using a rubber seal bearing his name, and a question regarding sufficiency of such a signing may arise if he adopts the same method when it comes to signing his will. It is well settled that if a testator signs his will by using a seal only, it will not be a sufficient signing unless the seal is authenticated by the addition of his initials (*In the Goods of Emerson* 9 L.R. Ir. 443). If it were otherwise, the door would be open to fraud. Although illiteracy is less of a problem nowadays, it never disqualified a person from making a will, and, for the purposes of signing his will, a person who is illiterate is allowed to make his mark as a valid signing. However, to be sufficient as a mark, it must be made in the form of an X, and the practice is that the X is made between the typed version of the testator's first name and surname (*Bennett v. Brumfitt* L.R. 3 C.P. 28; see *In the Goods of Kieran* [1933] I.R. 222).

The Testator Directing Another to Sign on His Behalf

2-03 Section 78 also presents a testator with the option of either signing himself or directing another person to sign on his behalf. This way of signing may be used by a testator who is so ill or physically incapacitated that he is unable to sign himself (see *Fulton v. Kee* [1961] N.I. 1). This option may also be exercised by an illiterate testator. A blind testator, however, has no option but to direct another to sign his will on his behalf.

The Testator Acknowledging His Signature

2-04 Where a testator has already signed his will in the absence of the witnesses, such a signing will be invalid unless he later acknowledges his signature in the presence of the two witnesses (Succession Act 1965, s.78, r.2). If a testator decides to acknowledge his signature instead of making a new one in the presence of the witnesses, he should be careful to inform the witnesses of this fact (*Kavanagh v. Fegan* [1932] I.R. 566). This may simply be done by the testator pointing at his signature and indicating that it is his signature. The witnesses must, however, have the opportunity of seeing his name or at least the opportunity of seeing it had they looked (*Hudson v. Parker* 1 Rob. 14). An acknowledgment after the witnesses have signed is invalid.

The Position of the Testator's Signature

2-05 A professionally drafted will usually concludes with the words "In Witness whereof I have hereunto signed my name the day and year first above written", and it is under these words that the testator signs his name. However, a great deal of leeway is given to the position of the testator's signature by section 78, rules 3 and 4, of the Succession Act 1965. So far as concerns the position of the signature of the testator or of the person signing for him under rule 1, rule 3 provides that it is sufficient if the signature is so placed at or after, or following, or under, or beside, or opposite to the end of the will that it is apparent on the face of the will that the testator intended to give effect, by the signature, to the writing signed as his will. Rule 4 provides that no such will shall be affected by the following circumstances:

(1)   the signature does not follow or is not immediately after the foot or end of the will;

(2)   a blank intervenes between the concluding word of the will and the signature;

(3) the signature is placed among words of the *testimonium* clauses or of the clause of attestation, either with or without a blank space intervening, or follows, or is after, or under, or beside the names or one of the names of the attesting witnesses;

(4) the signature is on a side or page or other portion of the paper or papers containing the will on which no clause or paragraph or disposing part of the will is written above the signature;

(5) there appears to be sufficient space on or at the bottom of the preceding side or page or other portion of the same paper on which the will is written to contain the signature.

The enumeration of the circumstances outlined above will not restrict the generality of rule 1.

Rule 5 provides that a signature will not be operative to give effect to any disposition or direction inserted after the signature is made. Where a will consists of a number of pages the signature need only appear on the last page (*In the Goods of Madden* [1905] 2 I.R. 612).

The Signing by the Witnesses

2-06 A will, in order to be duly executed, must be attested by two witnesses. An attestation clause stating that the two witnesses signed in the presence of the testator should appear below the space left for the testator's signature; otherwise, an affidavit of due execution may be required when probate is sought deposing that the provisions of section 78 of the Succession Act regarding due execution have been satisfied (Appendix 3, Form No. 1). An attestation clause may take the following form:

> "SIGNED PUBLISHED AND DECLARED by the said (*testator's name*) as and for his last Will and Testament in the presence of us who at his request and in his presence and in the presence of each other (all three being present at the same time) have hereunto subscribed our names as witnesses"

or simply

> "SIGNED by the Testator in our presence and signed by us in the presence of him (or her) and of each other".

If the testator acknowledges rather than signs in the presence of the witnesses, the attestation clause should state that he acknowledged his signature instead of signed. The meaning of the word "presence" for the purposes of the due execution of a will has been liberally interpreted by the courts, and has been interpreted to cover a variety of circumstances perhaps not normally associated with the everyday meaning of the word. For instance, in *Newton v. Clarke* 2 Curt. 320), the witnesses were deemed to have signed in the presence of a testator even though a bed curtain separated the testator and the witnesses. A similar finding was made in *Casson v. Dade* (1 Bro. Ch. C. 98), where a testatrix sat outside her solicitor's office but had the opportunity of seeing the witnesses sign had she looked. In yet another case, *Mulhall v. Mulhall* ([1936] I.R. 712), one of the witnesses left the room in which the testator signed his name, but, as the door remained open, he was in a position to see the testator sign had he cared to look. In the case of a blind testator, the witnesses must attest in such a way that if the testator had his sight, he would have been in a position to see them sign; however, the witnesses themselves must not be blind even if the testator had his sight. The wiser course to adopt is that the witnesses should remain in the immediate presence of the testator until the will is duly executed, thus placing beyond doubt the question of presence and preventing costly litigation to decide whether a fastidious testator or mobile witness was "present" at the time of execution. Finally, while it is essential that the two witnesses be jointly present when the testator signs his name, it is not necessary that the witnesses should sign in each other's presence although, as stated above, the wiser course would be for all three parties to remain present until the will is duly executed.

The Witnesses' Signatures

2-07 A witness must make his signature or mark with the intention of attesting the testator's signature. As in the case of a testator's signature, the courts have had to consider situations in which it was contended that a will was not properly attested. It was decided in *In the Estate of Bulloch* (1968] N.I. 96; see also *In the Goods of Garner* (1 L.R. Ir. 507) that a mark made by a witness with the intention of attesting was sufficient even though the witness was literate and able to sign his name. The initials of a witness will also be acceptable (see *Harrison v. Harrison* 8 Ves. 185). However, it will not suffice for a witness merely to go over a signature already made by him with a dry pen (*In the Goods of Maddoch* L.R. 3 P. & D. 169).

The Position of the Witnesses' Signatures

2-08 The witnesses should sign their names under the attestation clause, and although the signatures themselves will be sufficient, the practice is also to include their addresses primarily in case they should be required to testify in the event of a challenge to the will. Their occupations may also be added more as an embellishment than anything else. It is important to remember that a witness should be other than a beneficiary, as a gift to a witness or the spouse of a witness is void. However, a later marriage between a beneficiary and a witness will not render a gift void.

Presumption of Due Execution

2-09 Where a will appears to be properly signed and witnessed, it will be presumed that the statutory provisions regarding the due execution have been complied with. This useful presumption will continue to apply notwithstanding the subsequent death of a witness, or that a witness who is sought cannot be traced, or that a witness is unable to recall the circumstances surrounding the execution. Where, however, the testator's signature is called into question and there is some doubt regarding its authenticity, the court may refuse to apply the presumption. The Supreme Court considered the application of the presumption in *In the Estate of Early* ([1980] I.R. 223). In that case the deceased was an elderly man. He died in the house of a distant relative who had cared for him during his last years. His only assets consisted of a farm. Nearly two years after his death this distant relative produced a document purporting to be the will of the deceased leaving his farm to her. The document, although signed by the deceased and two witnesses, contained no attestation clause. The two witnesses were dead when the document was produced. The signature of one of the witnesses, who was a friend of the deceased, was identified by his widow. There was no evidence, however, verifying the signature of the deceased. The court was asked to apply the maxim *omnia praesumuntur rite et solemniter esse acta* to the circumstances surrounding the execution of the document. O'Higgins C.J. in his judgment thought that it was asking too much of the court to apply the presumption to the circumstances of the case. It was essential that evidence be adduced to show that the will was actually signed by the deceased. The evidence in support of the application established that the document was signed by one of the witnesses. Although the application of the presumption was also capable of carrying the apparent attestation of the second witness, since a person bearing that name and address existed and was a friend of the deceased, there was, however, a complete absence of any evidence to verify the signature "Hugh Early" as being that of the deceased. In fact, not only was there an absence of supportive evidence, there was also an allegation, though of doubtful authenticity, that the signature was not that of the deceased. Applying the presumption to the facts of the case, O'Higgins C.J., was of the view that two conditions must be observed:

"In the first place an intention to do some formal act must be established. In the second place there must be an absence of credible evidence that due formality was not observed. Here it can be said that the second condition is established. But what of the first? While the document has a testamentary flavour, it is established that it is not a holograph. In the absence of any evidence that it was signed by the deceased, there is no evidence of an intention on his part to enter into the formality of making a will."

The evidence was insufficient to justify the making of a grant.

The Principle of Knowledge and Approval

2-10 When a will is ready for execution the testator should be given the opportunity of reading it, or at least it should be read over to him in such a way that he understands the contents before it is executed. Where there is doubt regarding a testator's understanding of the contents, it may have to be established to the satisfaction of the court that he knew and approved of the contents before execution. Where a will is sought to be "propounded" or established by a person who prepared the will and who is also a major beneficiary, the court will view it with suspicion and may even pronounce against it unless the suspicion is removed. When the principle becomes an issue, it must be shown that the testator knew and approved of the contents either at the time of giving instructions or at the time of execution of the will. On either of these two dates a testator must know and approve of the contents of his will; this may be established where it is shown that a testator had read the will himself or that it was read over to him by another, perhaps by the person who prepared the will, so as to afford him the opportunity of confirming that the will truly reflects his wishes or of having certain matters arising out of the will explained to him more clearly; apparently, where this has been done at the instructions stage, it need not be repeated at the date of execution provided it is further established that he knew that he was executing a will. Order 79, rule 62, of the Rules of the Superior Courts must also be mentioned in this regard as it specifically requires that, in the case of a blind and illiterate testator, a grant of probate or letters of administration with the will annexed will not be allowed to issue by the probate officer unless he is satisfied by affidavit evidence that the will was read over to the testator before its execution, or that the testator had at such time knowledge of its contents. However, where the principle is raised as an issue, the circumstances surrounding a case will determine the approach to be adopted by the courts. Where it is shown that a will was procured and prepared by a person who was also a beneficiary or who had a benefit increased by a subsequent codicil, the vigilance of the court will be awakened and it will view such circumstances as suspicious, and the onus of proof will rest on such person to satisfy the court of the righteousness of the transaction. This onus may be discharged by adducing evidence which establishes that the testator knew and approved of the contents of the will at the time of execution. Where no such circumstances exist but yet there is some doubt as to whether a testator knew and approved of the contents owing to his state of health or age, the issue of whether he knew and approved may involve an evaluation of his intellectual capacity by the court. The evidence adduced will determine whether he had sufficient intellectual capacity to know and approve of the contents of his will, although, in this instance where such evidence is not forthcoming, the court may apply the presumption of testamentary capacity where a will has been duly executed. Also, in such a case where there is evidence forthcoming that a testator knew and approved of the *instructions* given for his will, this may be sufficient to satisfy the court that he knew and approved of the contents of his will "provided that the circumstances were such as would enable the Court to say that he knew the will had been drawn according to his instructions." Where a testator is merely confirming instructions already given with knowledge and approval, it may not be necessary to show that he knew and approved of contents at the time of execution, provided that he understood that he was executing a will. Furthermore, although section 77(1) of the Succession Act is expressed in the margin to deal with capacity to make a will, the expression "sound disposing mind" used in the section was held by McCarthy J. in *In the Goods of Glynn, Deceased: Glynn v. Glynn* ([1990] 2 I.R. 326) to be "a legislative adoption of a judicial term of art requiring that a testator should know and approve of the contents of the will and, at the time of execution of the will, be of sound mind, memory and understanding." Lynch J. in *In the Estate of Blackhall* (unreported Supreme Court, April 1, 1998) shared the same view. As a result of recent Supreme Court decisions in cases where there are no suspicious circumstances surrounding the knowledge and approval by a testator of the contents of his will, it seems that the main issue for the court to determine is whether the testator had sufficient intellectual appreciation of the contents of his will either at the time he gave the instructions for it or at the date of execution, especially where ill-health or old age is introduced as a vitiating element. A failure by a testator to have a sufficient intellectual appreciation to know and approve of the contents of his will may also result in a lack of testamentary capacity, as the expression "sound disposing mind" has been held to encapsulate the two.

Alterations

2-11 Section 86 of the Succession Act specifically deals with the question of alterations of wills, and provides that if the signature of the testator and the signature of each witness is made in the margin or on some other part of the will opposite or near the alteration, or at the foot or end of, or opposite to a memorandum referring to such alteration, and written at the end of some other part of the will, the alteration will be sufficiently executed. Order 79, rule 10, of the Rules of the Superior Courts also provides that interlineations and alterations appearing in a will are invalid unless they existed prior to its execution; or, if made afterwards, unless they were executed and attested in the mode required by law; or unless they were made valid by the re-execution of the will, or by a subsequent codicil to the will. Where alterations or inter-lineations are not duly executed, or cited or identified in the attestation clause, an affidavit in proof of their having existed in the will prior to its execution must be filed in the probate office. The court may also place reliance on the internal evidence furnished by the will. In *In the Goods of Benn* ([1938] I.R. 313) two lines of the will of the deceased testatrix were completely obliterated with a blue copying pencil and adhesive stamp paper leaving the underlying words indecipherable. There was also an interlineation in blue pencil noting a change of address of one of the legatees. The main question arose in respect of an interlineation in the principal disposition of the testatrix's property which appeared as follows:

> "and poperty [*sic*]

> The rest of my money/ I die seized or possessed of, to my sister Georgina, to be divided with her daughter as she thinks best."

A question arose as to whether the words "and poperty" were to be included in the grant of probate and whether the effect of their inclusion would also cover property owned by the testatrix other than her money. Hanna J. was of the opinion that, having regard to the internal evidence and the opinion of a handwriting expert, the words "and poperty" were inserted before execution. There was no direct evidence of any kind as to the time when the interlineation was made and there was no declaration of the testatrix before the execution of the will as to its contents or her interlineations. Therefore, the question arose as to how far he was entitled in law to rely on internal evidence and whether it was sufficient to draw an inference that the words "and poperty" were inserted before the execution of the will. Hanna J. held that the court could rely on its own judgment of the internal evidence as presented by the fabric of the will, and also on the evidence of handwriting experts on the appearance of the writing in the documents. Accordingly, he ordered that the words "and poperty" be admitted to probate and inserted in the grant.

Incorporation of Documents

2-12 Where documents are referred to in a will or codicil, then existing and clearly identified at the time of execution, and regardless whether they are themselves validly executed or not, they will form part of the will and will be admitted to probate with the will. It is most important, therefore, to prove that the documents existed at the time of execution, and that they are sufficiently and clearly identified by the words of incorporation. There are a number of decided cases where invalid testamentary instruments were the subject of incorporation. In *Woodroofe v. Creed* ([1894] 1 I.R. 508) a prior unattested codicil which was not referred to in a subsequent codicil was refused admission to probate with the will and subsequent codicil, having failed to satisfy the statutory rules regarding due execution, and could only have been salvaged by a proper incorporation which was not done. In *In the Goods of Wilmot* (1 Sw. & Tr. 36) a memorandum was written at the foot of a will before it was executed; however, after the execution of the will, it was found to be below the signatures of the testator and witnesses. A codicil to the will which was later executed did not refer to the memorandum. It was held that as there was no reference to it either in the will itself or in the subsequent codicil, it was excluded from probate. In *Re the Goods of Pearse* (L.R. 1 P. 382) as only one of three codicils was attested and there was no reference in the attested codicil to the unattested codicils, only the attested codicil was admitted to probate. Where there are a number of documents referred to in a will, and some of them cannot be found, only those found and proved to be in existence at the time of execution and duly incorporated can be admitted to probate. In *Newton v. Newton* (7 Ir. Jur. (N.S.) 129) it was held that parol evidence was admissible to identify the documents referred to in a will, but not to prove intention to incorporate. Even where the documents to be incorporated are validly executed documents themselves, the necessity of proving their identification and existence at the time of execution of the will remains, and clear words of incorporation must be used. In *In the Goods of the Countess of Durham* (3 Curt. 57) the testatrix incorporated by reference a revoked will made by her late husband, which was in existence, though not in her possession, at the time she made her will; it was entitled to be admitted to probate as part of her will. In *In the Goods of Darby* (4 N.C. 427) a testatrix in her will gave a gift to the same residuary legatees and on similar conditions to those in her father's will; it was held that this reference incorporated the relevant part of her father's will. Incorporation may also lead to the revival of parts of a revoked will, and the incorporation by a codicil may partially restore a revoked codicil. Even a foreign will may be incorporated by reference to it and included in the probate of the referring will.

Codicils

2-13 Codicils, although supplementary to the provisions of the main will, must comply with the statutory provisions contained in section 78 of the Succession Act 1965 in order to be valid. Codicils may be used for a variety of purposes concerning the contents of a will and may alter or revoke the contents of a former will by express reference to the will and the part to be altered or revoked, or by necessary implication. However, they may also have a more general application in that they may entirely revoke a present will or revive an earlier one by reference. Whatever their purpose, they must be duly executed in the same way as a will, and the same rules which are applicable to the testator's and witnesses' signatures and presence at the time of execution are similarly applicable to codicils.

The Liability of a Solicitor

2–14 Generally, a solicitor has a contractual duty to carry out his client's instructions and owes a duty to exercise reasonable care and skill in attending to his client's affairs. The whole question of a solicitor's contractual and tortious liability in relation to the preparation and execution of wills was considered by Sir Robert Megarry in *Ross v. Caunters* ([1980] Ch. 297). In that case it was held that if a solicitor is retained by a testator to draft and execute a will and the will confers a benefit on a named legatee, the solicitor must know that if he fails in his professional duty to draft and execute the will properly, a beneficiary will suffer loss. Therefore, a solicitor owes a duty of care in preparing and executing a will not only to the testator but also to a beneficiary and may be liable for any loss caused to a beneficiary by failing to observe the rules regarding the due execution of a will and resulting in a will being declared invalid. Barrington J. in *Wall v. Hegarty and Callanan* ([1980] I.L.R.M. 124) approved and adopted the judgment of Sir Robert Megarry in *Ross v. Caunters*.

A Will is Effective on Death Only

2-15 Since, unlike other legal instruments, a will does not take effect until the death of the testator, it is said to be "ambulatory". What this essentially means is that a testator is free to alter the provisions of his will by codicil during his lifetime or to revoke it totally. That a will should be ambulatory is understandable as there may be a considerable time lapse between the making of a will and the testator's death, and as more property may be acquired by the testator, he should be allowed to alter or revoke his will to dispose of this property by making a new will. Of course, a beneficiary may also predecease the testator and he may make a new will to take account of this. On the death of the testator, his will shall take effect and it will "speak" from that date.

CHAPTER 3

Capacity to Make a Will, Undue Influence and Fraud

Capacity

3–01 For a will to be valid it must not only be executed in compliance with section 78 of the Succession Act, it must also be made by a person who has the legal capacity to do so. Capacity basically involves two matters: age and mental condition of the testator. Section 77 of the Succession Act provides that for a person to make a valid will he must be at least 18 years and of sound disposing mind. Insofar as age is concerned, although there is a specified minimum age, there is no maximum age. Once the age of 18 years has been attained, a will cannot be invalidated on the grounds of age only. The other requirement – that a person have a "sound disposing mind" – may prove to be a difficult matter because the vagaries of the human mind are not subject to precise definition. A testator's mental condition may of course be impugned on the grounds of mental ill-health, but other factors, such as the effects of old age and physical ill-health, may also introduce some doubt regarding the mental condition of a particular testator. While old age and ill-health alone will not deprive a person of capacity, the effect of such on a person's mental well-being may result in the loss of capacity.

Age of the Testator

3-02 For the purposes of section 77 a testator must have attained the age of 18 years, or, where under that age, must be married or must have been married. This replaced section 7 of the Wills Act 1837, which required that a testator be 21 years old at the time of making his will. Prior to the Marriages Act 1972, the age requirement for marriage was 12 years for a girl and 14 years for a boy. Section 1(1) of the 1972 Act increased the age to 16 years for both sexes. Thus the marriage of persons over the age of 16 and under the age of 18 years will entitle them to make a valid will. However, the marital age is now 18 years for both parties, so the special category provided by section 77 for married persons is no longer relevant.

Sound Disposing Mind

3-03 The expression "sound disposing mind" used in section 77 is a legal expression and not a medical one. Although medical evidence may be adduced to assist the court in ascertaining the state of mind of a testator at the time of making his will, such evidence may not be conclusive. A testator's mind must be "sound" when it comes to the disposition of his property by will. It was stated in Sir J. Hannen in *Boughton v. Knight* (L.R. 3 P. & D. 64 at 65) that:

> "The testator's mind must be sound to be capable of forming the testamentary intentions embodied in the will; his memory must be sound to recall the several persons who ought to be considered as his possible beneficiaries; his understanding must be sound so that he may comprehend their various ties with him by blood or friendship, and their claims on these or other grounds upon his testamentary bounty."

And in "disposing" of his property by will:

> "It is essential . . . that a testator shall understand the nature of his act and its effects; shall understand the extent of his property he is disposing; shall be able to comprehend and appreciate the claims to which he ought to give effect, and, with a view to the latter object, that no disaster of mind shall poison his affections, pervert his sense of right, or prevent the exercise of his natural faculties, that no insane delusion shall influence his will in disposing his property and bring about a disposal of it which, if his mind had been sound, would not have made."

It may be clear from the beginning that a person does not possess sufficient intellectual understanding of the nature of a will because of mental retardation from birth, or later because of mental impairment resulting, for instance, from brain damage sustained in an accident reducing him to such a vegetative state that there is no question of his being capable of making a will. However, in less obvious cases, where a person's mind is impaired as a result of physical or mental illness, it may be a question of whether or not he possesses a sufficient degree of understanding to make a will. But the courts generally are loathe to hold against a will, even where a testator is shown to be labouring under severe physical disabilities and has difficulties in communicating, once he has sufficient mental capacity and manages somehow to communicate his testamentary wishes (*Gillet v. Rogers* 108 L.T. 732). Also, a deterioration in mental health between the time when the testator instructs his solicitor to prepare his will and the time of the execution of his will, will not necessarily deprive him of testamentary capacity: a slight degree of mental capacity is required to complete the execution of his will (*Parker v. Felgate* 8 P.D. 171; see also *Perera v. Perera* [1901] A.C. 354).

Mental Ill-Health

3–04 Whenever mental ill-health is alleged to invalidate a will, the onus of proof lies on the party making the allegation to establish that the testator's mind was so affected by it that he was incapable of making a valid will. It is not so much that a testator suffered from mental ill-health at the time of execution of the will, but rather that it was so severe as to deprive him of testamentary capacity over a period of time. The effect of ill-health on a testator's capacity was considered by McCarthy J. in *In the Goods of Glynn, Deceased: Glynn v. Glynn* ([1990] 2 I.R. 326). The facts of that case were that the testator died on February 14, 1982, at the age of 77. He suffered a massive stroke on October 5, 1981, and was thereafter confined to hospital. He executed his will on October 20. On that day, without obtaining any medical advice, the witnesses concluded that the testator knew what he was doing and was capable of making a will. One of the witnesses drew up the will in accordance with the deceased's instructions. He left all his property to a second cousin with whom he had no connection other than that they both shared the same family name, and excluded his elder sister who was unmarried and who lived all her life with him on the family farm. Neither of the witnesses was a beneficiary in the will. The testator's doctor, however, was of the opinion that the testator was "disorientated" on the day he executed the will. He also concluded that the testator's level of consciousness was such that he was unable to communicate any of his own ideas and that some method of communication would first have to be devised for him, "some code whereby he understood and agreed that the ideas that were being communicated to him coincided with his own ideas." Another doctor was of the same opinion. The question was whether his state of ill-health deprived him of testamentary capacity. McCarthy J. held that the deceased in the present case was merely confirming instructions already given and that he was told truthfully that the document represented what he had expressed to be his testamentary wishes, and as the two witnesses were quite satisfied that he knew what he was doing, the will was a valid one. However, where a person is diagnosed as suffering from a particular mental illness, as a result of which his mind cannot be said to be sound, testamentary incapacity will be the inevitable consequence. Certain types of mental illness have been given more sympathetic consideration by the court than others, and the existence of such may not be found to have deprived a person of testamentary capacity. For instance, where it is shown that the testator was subject to an insane delusion, the first approach of the court is to treat it with great distrust and every presumption should be made against it. Although the general presumption of sanity will be applied by the court, this may be reversed where it is established that a testator has been diagnosed as being mentally ill and is undergoing treatment for it. For instance, where a person has been diagnosed as a paranoid schizophrenic, and even though such a mental condition is incurable, he may still have capacity to make a will, where it is established that the condition can be effectively controlled by the use of medication (*O'Donnell v. O'Donnell*, unreported, High Court, Kelly J., March 24, 1999). The mental condition of senile dementia is a condition associated with old age, although there is the rather rare condition of premature senility which may affect a person who is not elderly. It is manifested mainly by a testator being unable to remember recent events in his life. As one of the prerequisites of a sound disposing mind includes that of memory, it is the memory of the testator which will be in question where senility is alleged. While the ravages of age may be visited upon the entire mind of a person, senility leads to a particular disintegration of the memory. The decision in *Duffy v. Kearney and Duffy* (unreported, High Court, O'Hanlon August 10, 1994) is a good example of the approach taken by the court to the evidence given at a trial involving testamentary capacity. In that case the testator was a bachelor who lived alone on a farm in close proximity to his brother, Vincent Duffy, the plaintiff, who also farmed in the same locality. The defendants were a sister and brother of the deceased who had left Ireland and went to live in the United States many years before the death of the deceased and who made only occasional visits to Ireland prior to his death. The testator left his farm to the plaintiff. At the time of making his will, however, he was extremely ill in hospital, which caused the defendants to have doubts about his capacity to make a will. As a result of such doubts, they entered a caveat, which eventually led to a full probate action challenging the validity of the will made by the deceased. O'Hanlon J., in the course of his judgment, considered the evidence given by a medical expert and the solicitor who prepared the deceased's will regarding the mental capacity of the deceased at the date of execution of the will. Although he stated that the evidence of the medical expert had to be treated with respect, he nevertheless went on to say that:

> "what he had to say about the general effect of the human intellect and perception of personal relationships and affairs of administration of drugs of the type which were administered to the deceased during his last illness . . . was not, in my opinion, sufficient to dislodge the very comprehensive evidence given by Mr. O'Carroll, Solicitor, and by the other witnesses who visited and conversed [with the deceased]."

The solicitor knew the deceased and had acted for the deceased's family for a long period before the will was made. The evidence of the deceased's solicitor as to the general physical and mental state of the deceased was strongly supported by the evidence of the other witnesses who visited him in hospital around the time of execution of the will and the general conclusions of another medical practitioner about the capacity of the deceased. O'Hanlon J.

had no difficulty in declaring in favour of the will and finding that the deceased testator was of sound disposing mind.

Undue Influence

3–05 The parties and circumstances surrounding the making of a will may also become the subject of the court's scrutiny where it is alleged that the testator was unduly influenced when making his will. In other words, the allegation in this instance is that the will made by the testator was not freely made by him. Where the volition of a testator is alleged to have been suppressed, the degree of pressure exerted by the person alleged to have applied it will be considered by the court to see the effect it had on the testator. Was the testator in question influenced by the kind of pressure exerted? The leading authorities on the matter have set down the parameters at persuasion only and anything beyond that would be considered pressure, the essential ingredient of undue influence (*Hall v. Hall* L.R. 1 P. & D. 481; *Wingrove v. Wingrove* 11 P.D. 81; see also *Re Kavanagh*; *Healy v. Mac Gillycuddy and Lyons* [1978] I.L.R.M. 175). The onus of proof lies on the party who alleges the existence of undue influence, and the evidence adduced must establish that not only was influence exerted by a particular party but that it was undue and that it affected the testator's will.

Fraud

3-06 Fraud eludes definition. Indeed, so varied are the acts that may constitute fraud that any attempt to define it would bind the hands of the courts in their efforts to counter newly-devised fraudulent schemes. There are no rules specifying what acts constitute a fraud for the purposes of rendering a will invalid, although the relevant time for ascertaining the presence of an act which is alleged to be fraudulent is the time when the testator makes his will. Fraud is a separate plea to undue influence and cannot be raised directly under a plea of undue influence.

CHAPTER 4

The Revocation and Revival of Wills

Revocation

4-01 It has already been observed that a will is ambulatory until death (see Chapter 2, para. 2-15). However, between the making of a will and death, there is a time period, which may be great or small. If a testator is capable of making a valid will at any time after the age of 18 years, it would be ludicrous to hold a testator bound by a will made at that age to take effect on death, which, given a reasonable expectation of life, may occur many years later, to take an extreme case. Therefore, the right of a testator to revoke his will at any time during his lifetime is a necessary corollary of the ambulatory nature of a will. In fact, revocation is an inevitable consequence of making a will; any attempt to make a will irrevocable will not be countenanced by the courts.

Methods of Revocation

4-02 There are three methods of revocation recognised by section 85 of the Succession Act 1965: one, by the subsequent marriage of the testator; two, by a testamentary instrument (including "some writing" executed in testamentary form); and three, by a testator destroying his will. Therefore, a will may be revoked by a valid ceremony of marriage, by a new will revoking an earlier one, or by the destruction of an earlier will.

Revocation by Subsequent Marriage

4-03 Once the marriage of the testator is duly solemnised, any former will or codicil is thereby revoked. The subsequent marriage automatically revokes the will and there is no necessity to show an intention to revoke. The marriage must, however, be a valid one, and if, owing to the presence of a vitiating element, it is rendered void, it will not revoke a former will. Where owing to the presence of a vitiating element the marriage is shown to be a voidable one, the marriage will continue to subsist, and will not be sufficient to revoke a former will unless it is subsequently annulled by the courts. A voidable marriage once annulled has retrospective effect to the date of the marriage, thus allowing a former will to be reinstated as the will of the testator whose marriage has been annulled from that date.

A Will Made in Contemplation of Marriage

4-04 Section 85(1) further provides that a will made in contemplation of a subsequent marriage, whether so expressed in the will or not, will not be revoked by that marriage. Thus, where a will is made by the testator prior to the ceremony of marriage, but in contemplation of that marriage, the subsequent marriage of the testator will not revoke that will, even though no express mention of the testator's forthcoming marriage appears on the face of the will. Obviously, where there is no mention of a marriage in the will, sufficient evidence will have to be adduced proving that the will was made in contemplation of it. In *Pilot v. Gainfort* ([1931] P. 103) the testator had previously been married to a woman who had left him a number of years before he made his will and who was not seen or heard of for more than seven years, thus allowing for the presumption of death; he bequeathed the whole of his estate to a woman with whom he was living and whom he described as his "wife"; shortly after he had made his will, he had married this woman. The court held that the testator's marriage to this woman was *prima facie* a sufficient description of her as his wife, and that he had made his will in contemplation of marriage to her. Lord Merrivale, at page 104, said:

> "Under the circumstances I do not think that it can be doubted that the will was in contemplation of the subsequent marriage and practically expresses that contemplation and is good."

(See also *Sallis v. Jones* [1935] P. 43; *In the Estate of Gray* [1963] 107 S.J. 156).

Revocation by Destruction

4-05 To constitute a valid revocation by destruction of a will the physical act of destruction must be accompanied by an intention to revoke the will. It was aptly said by one judge that "all the destroying in the world without intention will not revoke a will, nor all the intention in the world without destroying; there must be the two" (*Cheese v. Lovejoy* 2 P.D. 251 at 263 *per* James L.J.). Thus, the act of destruction and the intention to revoke must exist together at the time of revocation.

The Act of Destruction

4-06 Section 85(2) of the Succession Act 1965 provides that the physical act of destruction may take the form of a burning, tearing, or otherwise destroying. Any of these forms of destruction may be used to revoke a will either totally or partially. In the latter event, where a testator intends to destroy part of his will only, the remainder in its mutilated form may be admitted to probate. In addition to burning or tearing, other acts of destruction which assail the essence of the will, namely, the writing, will also be acceptable, and it will be the writing which will be subject-matter for debate by the courts, and not the material upon which a will is made, although in reality both the writing and the material are usually destroyed by the same act of destruction. To destroy one without the other may sound more like the act of the magician rather than of law, but there are a number of instances where this can happen – for instance, where the testator completely erases a will written in pencil. Other instances have involved the scratching out or severing by the testator of his signature from his will (*In the Goods of White* 3 L.R. Ir. 413), or the erasure by the testator of the signatures of the attesting witnesses (*Margarry v. Robinson* 12 P.D. 8). An act of destruction is irreversible and any later attempt by a testator to restore his will to its original form, even if that is possible, will not be viewed as a revival of the instrument (see *Bell v. Fothergill* L.R. 2 P. 148).

The Intention to Revoke

4-07 The intention to revoke is essential to an effective revocation. The act without the intent will not suffice. Further, if there is some doubt about the mental capacity of the testator to form the necessary intention, it must be shown to the satisfaction of the court that he was capable of forming the necessary intention, and the same evidence required to show the testamentary capacity of a testator will be required here also. A testator who destroys his will while being of unsound mind, will not revoke his will (*In the Goods of Hine* [1893] P. 282). A will which is destroyed by mistake will also not be a valid revocation as it is not done with the intention of revoking it, for instance, where a testator destroys his will because he believes it to be useless (see *Stamford v. White* [1901] P. 46), or where he thought that "he was merely disposing of rubbish" (Re Jones [1976] Ch. 200 at 205). The testator must have more than the intention to destroy his will, he must also have the intention to revoke it.

By Inference

4-08 While a meticulous testator may solemnly declare before witnesses that the will he is about to destroy is done with the intention of revoking and this is the ideal revocation, there is something less calculating about revocation by destruction than by a formal revocation by will. In the heat of a moment a testator may take out his will and either destroy it totally or partially, having decided as a result of a recent argument with his beneficiaries that they are no longer deserving of his bounty. The question then arises whether he destroyed his will with the intention of revoking or simply out of pique. However, whatever emotion may have led a testator to destroy his will, will only be of legal concern where it helps to establish the intention of revocation by inference or otherwise. The nature and extent of the destruction may lead the court to draw certain inferences in deciding whether the testator had the requisite intention to destroy his will totally or partially, or, indeed, whether he had intended to destroy it at all (*In the Goods of White* 3 L.R. Ir. 413).

By Presumption

4-09 In the absence of being able to produce the will before the court to allow it to draw inferences from its condition, the court may have to rely on certain presumptions to help ascertain the intention of the testator. The court may presume, where a will is not found after the death of the testator, and where it was last known to be in his possession, that it was destroyed with the intention of revoking it, but only after a reasonable search for it has been carried out and due enquiries have been made as to its whereabouts. The basis of the presumption is that a document like a will would be carefully deposited by a testator in a secure place, and if the evidence discloses that the testator was a man who was cautious by nature in his everyday life and that it would have been uncharacteristic of him to treat important matters, such as his will, in a casual way, the presumption of revocation will prevail. For instance, in *In the Goods of Paget* (47 I.L.T.R. 284) the testator made his will and kept it carefully in his possession. Some years later he asked his daughter to get it from a drawer in which it was safely kept for the purposes of assuring himself that it was properly executed. On that occasion he expressed satisfaction with the terms of his will. No member of the testator's family ever saw the will again. On his death all his papers were found in good order, though the will was not among them. The court presumed that the testator had destroyed his will with the intention of revoking it.

Revocation by Testamentary Instrument

4-10 All professionally drafted wills contain a revocation clause which has immediate effect upon execution of the will. It is usually found at the beginning of a will following the name and address of the testator and may take the following form:

> "I (*name and address of testator*) make this as and for my last will and testament and hereby revoke all former wills and other testamentary dispositions heretofore made by me."

However, there is no set formula of words required by law, and any words used will be acceptable as long as the intention to revoke former wills is clearly expressed.

4-11 The revoking instrument need not take the form of a testamentary instrument, nor does it have to dispose of property. It will be sufficient if it consists of some written declaration made by the testator revoking a former will, although such writing must be duly executed like a will. It may take the form of a letter, although such a letter will differ from an ordinary letter in the sense that it must be executed like a will. In *In the Goods of Eyre* ([1905] 2 I.R. 540), a letter sent by the testatrix to her daughter which was duly signed and attested and which directed her daughter to destroy her will was held to be a valid instrument of revocation.

4-12 It may happen that on the death of a testator two wills are discovered, each purporting to be his last will. It is axiomatic that a testator shall not die leaving two wills, or as Swineburne said, "No man can die with two testaments." A testator is entitled to make as many wills as he pleases, and if they contain no revocation clauses they will all be taken together as his last will. As seen above a testator may replace a former will by expressly revoking it by a later will. But what if there are two wills duly executed and only the earlier will contains a revocation clause – which of them shall prevail? The answer will depend on the intention of the testator, and this will be ascertained by the court by examining the contents of the two wills and by taking into account the facts surrounding the making of them. The court may hold in favour of one of them because it is established in evidence that it was the later of the two, or may hold in favour of the earlier one because of the extent of the dispositions it contains in comparison to the later, and where a decision in favour of the later would be tantamount to the erstwhile testator dying intestate. However, where the two wills contain a revocation clause, and no evidence is adduced to show which was the later, and both contain substantial inconsistencies regarding the disposition of the testator's property, an intestacy will result.

Revocation Resulting in Intestacy

4-13 Where the two wills of the testator are substantially inconsistent and irreconcilable, and there is no evidence showing which was the first in time, and each contains a revocation clause, the court will refuse to grant probate of either will, and the testator will be deemed to have died intestate. In *In the Goods of Millar* ([1931] I.R. 364) a testatrix executed two wills on the same day. No evidence was adduced proving priority. The provisions of the wills were consistent in some respects, but inconsistent in others. Each will contained a revocation clause. As a result, the court refused to grant probate of either will.

Revocation by Codicil

4-14 Section 85(2) of the Succession Act 1965 also provides that a codicil duly executed may revoke a will. However, a codicil which revokes a former will does not necessarily revoke a prior codicil, although there may be an implied revocation of all prior or intermediate codicils. Because of its supplementary nature, a codicil will be construed as interfering as little as possible with the will: its very existence may depend on the will to which it refers (see Re Stoodley [1916] 1 Ch. 242.). However, as a codicil is also a testamentary instrument in its own right, the safer course to adopt when revoking a will is to ensure that all prior and intermediate codicils are also revoked by reference to them.

The Doctrine of Dependent Relative Revocation

4-15 Where a will is totally revoked by a later will or codicil, or by some writing executed like a will, or by an act of destruction, with the intention of revoking it, the revocation is absolute, and the former will ceases to exist. It was said by Kenny J. in *In the Goods of Irvine* ([1919] 2 I.R. 485) that "[i]f the act of revocation, whether by another will duly executed or by the destruction of the existing will, be without reference to any other act or event, the revocation may be an absolute one." However, if it is intended by the testator that the act of revocation is dependent on a subsequent will being validly made, the act of revocation of a former will, will be conditional on the validity of the subsequent will, and if the subsequent will fails to come into existence, or fails to be a valid instrument, the former will shall be treated as the will of the testator. In *West v. West* ([1921] 2 I.R. 34), the testator executed a will in February 1913. He died on September 9, 1919. After his death the will could not be found. An envelope which was found among his papers contained the message "my will made Jan 26, 1918, one made February, 1913, destroyed". The envelope contained a signed but unattested testamentary writing dated January 26, 1918, which was found to be based on a will made by the testator in February 1913. A copy of that will was produced by the testator's solicitors and was put in evidence as constituting the contents of a destroyed will. Probate in solemn form was sought by the executor of that will. The court held that the destruction of the will of February 1913 was conditional on the testator's belief that the testamentary writing dated January 26, 1918, would be effective as a will and, as that instrument failed as a will, the doctrine of dependent relative revocation was applicable. Accordingly, the contents of the will of February 1913 should be admitted to probate.

Revival of Wills

4-16 If the revival of a former will is successful, that will, together with the reviving instrument, will be admitted to probate. There are only two ways by which a will may be revived and they are set out in section 87 of the Succession Act 1965. Section 87 provides that:

> "No will or any part thereof, which is in any manner revoked, shall be revived otherwise than by the re-execution thereof or by a codicil duly executed and showing an intention to revive it…"

Revival by Re-Execution

4-17 Revival by re-execution occurs where the whole or part of a revoked will is executed afresh by the testator in compliance with the rules for making a new will. The only difference between the revival of a former revoked will by re-execution and the making of a new will is one of intention: in the former, the intention to revive a revoked will must be present at the date of execution of the reviving instrument, whilst in the latter, the intention is to make a new will. However, the mere revocation of a current will does not automatically revive an earlier will; a testator who assumes this runs the risk of dying intestate. If the revival of a former revoked instrument is intended by the testator, he must use one of the methods by which wills are revived under section 87. Perhaps, the more prudent approach is to make a new will incorporating the provisions of the will which the testator wishes to revive, thus putting beyond doubt what constitutes the will and avoiding any costly litigation testing the use of the revival rules.

Revival by Codicil

4-18 For a will to be revived by a codicil, the intention to revive must be expressed in the reviving codicil, or it may be implied from the nature of the gifts contained in it which would make it inconsistent with any other intention, or by the use of any other expression which would allow the court to conclude with reasonable certainty that the testator intended by codicil to revive a former will. The reviving codicil must also be accurate in identifying the will to be revived by it, and the courts will be slow to correct any inaccuracies in this respect.

CHAPTER 5

Testamentary Gifts, Statutory Rights and Claims

Testamentary Gifts

5-01 A gift, in order to be effective, must identify the property which is to form the subject-matter and the person who is the object. The nature of the gift will be determined by its subject-matter, *i.e.* whether it is a legacy or a devise. Once the nature of the gift has been ascertained, it must be shown to have complied with the rules creating such a gift. This may also involve determining whether the gift bears income or interest from a particular date. The value of a gift and the relationship of the beneficiary to the testator will further determine the extent of the beneficiary's liability to pay inheritance tax.

Classification of Testamentary Gifts

5-02 Testamentary gifts can be either a devise, a legacy, or a bequest. A devise is a gift of real property in a will, and it may be either specific or residuary. A specific devise is a gift of a particular parcel of real property, while a residuary devise is a gift of all remaining real property not otherwise specifically disposed of by the will. A legacy or bequest is a gift of personal property in a will, and it also may be specific or residuary, although legacies are subject to further classification. A specific legacy is a gift of a particular item of personal property or a certain sum of money, while a residuary legacy is a gift of all of a testator's remaining personal property or money not otherwise specifically disposed of in the will. Section 3(1) of the Succession Act 1965 provides that a pecuniary legacy includes an annuity, a general legacy, a demonstrative legacy so far as it is not discharged out of the designated property, and any other general direction by a testator for the payment of money, including all death duties, free from which any devise, bequest, or payment is made to take effect. A pecuniary legacy, therefore, consists of three further types of legacy other than a specific legacy, *viz.* a general legacy, a demonstrative legacy, and an annuity. Whether a legacy is specific or general is primarily a question of construction for the court: if the words used in creating the legacy are ambiguous, the court, when construing a legacy, will lean in favour of a conclusion that the legacy was a general legacy. A general legacy presupposes that the estate of the testator has sufficient assets to pay out the legacy. However, where a legacy consists of a money payment, the amount will be payable out of the realised assets of the deceased, unless the particular source of payment of the legacy has been indicated by the testator; if the testator knew at the time when he made his will that the source of payment indicated consists of the precise amount mentioned in the legacy, then it will be a specific legacy, for instance, where a legacy of a specified sum of money is payable out of a repository indicated by the testator in his will and consisting of the precise amount. A general legacy may also consist of a gift of shares in a company where a number of shares are given to a legatee, unless the testator owns a specific number of shares and gives them to the legatee as "my" shares followed by the amount of shares owned by the testator in that particular company, *viz.* "my 1000 shares in X plc". A demonstrative legacy indicates the actual fund out of which they are to be paid or the particular part of the property of the deceased from which they are to be taken. For instance, a particular bank account may be indicated from which the legacy must be paid or a particular shareholding in a company out of which a number of shares are to be given. Although a particular fund or a particular part of property is indicated for payment or discharge, a demonstrative legacy is also general in effect. In fact, a demonstrative legacy must be general in effect, otherwise it may be deemed a specific legacy which is payable out of a fund indicated by the testator, especially so, where that fund contains the exact amount for the payment of the legacy. An annuity is a legacy consisting of a periodic or yearly payment of a sum of money from income arising out of a particular part of the testator's property, usually to be paid out of property in the residuary estate of the testator. Usually, an annuity is intended as a source of income for the life of the legatee, although it may be construed as being limited in duration.

5-03 Property is traditionally divided into real and personal property, and although it may seem incongruous, leasehold property is a form of personal property known as chattels real. This traditional classification of property, however, is not used for succession purposes by the Succession Act 1965 where all the deceased's property is treated as his "estate". "Estate" by virtue of section 3(1) must be construed in accordance with section 14 of the 1965 Act. Section 14 provides that, for the purposes of the Act, the estate of the deceased person shall, unless a contrary intention appears, include references to both his real and personal estate. Section 3(1) provides that "real estate" has the meaning assigned to it by section 4 of the Act, and section 4(a) provides that "real estate" includes chattels real, and land in possession, remainder, or reversion, and every estate or interest in or over land. Since the Succession Act, a gift of a testator's whole estate includes both his real and personal property unless a contrary intention appears, and a gift of his real estate includes leaseholds as well (Succession Act 1965, s.4(a)). Further, by section 92 of the Act a general devise of land will be construed to include leasehold interests, unless a contrary intention appears in his will. Thus, where a testator intends to make a gift of his personal estate to include his leasehold interests, this should be specified in his will, otherwise, any gift of his real estate will be taken to include his leasehold interests, unless a contrary intention is expressed in his will.

Failure of Testamentary Gifts

5-04 A testamentary gift may fail to take effect on the following grounds:

(1) failure of the subject-matter of the gift;

(2) failure of the object of the gift;

(3) failure by act of a beneficiary; and

(4) failure for uncertainty.

(1) Failure of the Subject-matter of the Gift

5-05 This occurs where the subject-matter of the gift is disposed of by the testator during his lifetime, leaving nothing for the beneficiary to inherit. A beneficiary may be given a specific legacy in the will, for instance, a particular item of personal property, which is sold during the lifetime of the testator, or may be devised a specific parcel of land which is disposed of during the lifetime of the testator; thus, the specific legacy or devise is emptied of all content and nothing is left for the beneficiary to take. If such is the case, the gift is said to fail by way of ademption. However, ademption applies only to specific legacies and devises, and not to general or demonstrative legacies. For instance, a specific gift of money in a numbered account in a particular bank may be adeemed if the account is empty at the testator's death; a gift of money without identifying a source of payment will not be adeemed as it will be payable out of the general estate of the deceased; and a demonstrative gift of money will likewise be saved from ademption where it is expressed to be payable out of all the bank accounts of the deceased; in the latter case the source of payment is indicated but without specifically nominating any particular account for payment. The ademption of specific legacies of shares in a company is less clear than that of specific pecuniary legacies. No difficulty arises where the legacy consists of specific shares in a particular company which no longer exist at the date of death of the testator because the testator sold them during his lifetime. However, if the legacy consists of shares in a company which changes its name and this is followed by a change in the value of the shares because they are transformed into smaller denominations, the legacy may not be adeemed if it is shown that the essence of the legacy remains the same (*Re Clifford* [1912] 1 Ch. 29). A similar conclusion may be reached where the company in which the testator held shares is reconstructed after voluntary liquidation (*Re Lemming* [1912] 1 Ch. 665).

(2) Failure of the Object of the Gift

5-06 Where a gift lacks an object or beneficiary it lapses and ceases to have effect. The simplest exposition of this doctrine is where the beneficiary of a gift predeceases the testator. On such an event occurring, the destiny of the subject-matter of the gift will depend on the will itself or the relationship of the beneficiary to the testator. If the will of the testator contains a residuary gift, any gift which lapses through lack of an object will fall into residue, but where there is no residuary gift, then the lapsed gift will be distributed on a partial intestacy in accordance with the rules of intestacy. However, this will not happen if the predeceased beneficiary is a child or other issue of the testator who leaves issue of his own surviving at the time of death of the testator, as his issue will become entitled to the gift in his stead and it will not lapse unless a contrary intention appears from the will (Succession Act 1965, s.98).

(3) Failure by Act of a Beneficiary

5-07 A beneficiary himself, unwittingly or otherwise, may cause the failure of gift to him. He may do this by disclaiming the gift left to him or he may exclude himself from taking a gift by subscribing his name as a witness to the will. A person who signs his name below the signature of the testator is presumed to be an attesting witness to the will and a testamentary gift given either to him or his spouse, or any person claiming under him or his spouse, will "be utterly null and void" (Succession Act 1965, s.82).

(4) Failure for Uncertainty

5-08 Where the words used in creating a testamentary gift do not sufficiently identify the subject-matter, the gift will fail for uncertainty. The courts can only go as far as the rules of construction will allow them to go when attempting to save a gift, or, indeed, the will itself. However, the attitude of the courts is that a person would not make a will in the first place if he intended to die intestate, and the courts will, therefore, lend their assistance as far as possible in supporting his testamentary wishes. The courts will read the will so as to lead to a testacy, not an intestacy. This is the "golden rule"

(*Re Harrison* 30 Ch.D. 390). It is also a statutory rule that when "the purport of a devise or bequest admits of more than one interpretation, then, in case of doubt, the interpretation according to which the devise or bequest will be operative will be preferred" (Succession Act 1965, s.99).

Income

5-09 A beneficiary will become entitled to income arising from a gift which takes immediate effect on the death of the testator. Thus, in the case of a specific or residuary gift which takes effect immediately on the death of the testator, income arising from such gifts will accrue from that time. The subject-matter of a gift will determine the income accruing; for instance, where shares in a company are the subject-matter of a gift, any dividends declared on them will be viewed as income arising from such shares, and if the subject-matter is land, then any rents or profits arising out of the land will be treated as income and the beneficiary will become entitled to such income accordingly (*Re West* [1909] 2 Ch. 180). However, the right to receive income from gifts having immediate effect is accompanied by any liability which may also arise out of ownership of such gifts: thus, if a beneficiary assumes the mantle of a landlord by virtue of a gift having immediate effect, he will be entitled to receive any rent arising out of property, the subject-matters of the gift, but the concomitant duties of a landlord to his tenant in relation to the maintenance and upkeep of property will also follow (*Re Pearce* [1909] 1 Ch. 819), with the sole exception of contracts entered into by the testator prior to his death for the repair of premises, the costs of which will have to be borne by the testator's estate and not by the beneficiary (*Re Day's W.T.* [1962] 1 W.L.R. 1419).

Interest

5-10 The general rule is that interest accrues on gifts from the time they become payable. The type of gifts on which interest accrues are of course pecuniary legacies; other types of bequests by virtue of their nature, for instance, a suite of antique furniture, are not capable of bearing interest. The time for the payment of a pecuniary legacy is at the end of the executor's year, *i.e.* one year from the death of the testator. A testator may, however, direct in his will that a legacy be payable at an earlier time and such a direction also commences the accrual of interest from that time. He may, for instance, direct that a legacy becomes payable from the date of his death and such a direction also commences the accrual of interest. Moreover, certain legacies automatically bear interest from the date of death and do not require a direction by the testator in his will to this effect. If a legacy is given in satisfaction of a debt it will carry interest from the date of the testator's death and not from the end of the executor's year (*Re Rattenbury* [1906] 1 Ch. 667). However, the payment of such interest may be subject to a contrary intention expressed by the testator in his will by making the legacy in satisfaction of the debt payable from a particular date after his death and interest will accrue from that time only (*Adams v. Lavander* M'Cl. & Y. 41). Legacies given to children of the testator or to children to whom the testator stands *in loco parentis* and who are under the age of majority will also carry interest from the date of the testator's death, the underlying presumption being that the interest will be applied towards the maintenance of such children (*Re Bowlby* [1904] 2 Ch. 685). This presumption, however, will not be applied where trustees are appointed for such children who are invariably empowered anyway to provide for the maintenance of children (*Re Pollock* [1943] Ch. 338).

Inheritance Tax

5-11 Inheritance tax was first introduced into this country by the Capital Acquisitions Tax Act 1976, and is paid on the taxable value of every taxable inheritance taken by a successor of a deceased person. For this purpose a taxable inheritance means a tax payable on all property contained in the inheritance or gift made by a disponer (testator or intestate).

Disponer and Successor

5-12 A disponer means the person who provides the property contained in the disposition by will or share on intestacy. A successor is a person who becomes beneficially entitled to possession of property on the death of the disponer otherwise than for full valuable consideration in money or money's worth. A disposition includes a testamentary disposition, a share on total or partial intestacy, payment of the legal right share of a surviving spouse, or the making of provision for a surviving spouse or child of the deceased person under section 56 or section 117 of the Succession Act 1965.

Market Value

5-13 The value of property inherited is the basis for determining a beneficiary's liability to pay tax, and the value of the property calculated for this purpose is called the market value. The market value of any property is the price the property would fetch if sold in the open market on the date the property is

subject to valuation and it will be based on the best price reasonably obtaina-
ble by a vendor of such property. The valuation of agricultural property is
calculated in a different way. For a beneficiary to qualify for agricultural
relief as a farmer, not less than 80 per cent of the market value of the property
to which a beneficiary is entitled in possession must consist of agricultural
property. The valuation date of a taxable inheritance is the date on which an
executor or administrator, or, indeed, trustee, is entitled to retain the subject-
matter of the inheritance for the benefit of the successor or beneficiary, or the
date on which the subject-matter of the inheritance is so retained, or the date
of delivery, payment or other satisfaction or discharge of the subject-matter to
the successor or beneficiary. Inheritance tax is, therefore, charged on the market value of the property forming part of the inheritance on the valuation
date.

Computing Tax

5-14 Inheritance tax is computed on the basis of class thresholds and the
value of a threshold depends on the degree of relationship between the disponer and successor. There are three different group thresholds:

Group A: €422,148, where the successor is, on the day the gift of inheritance is taken, a parent, a child, or a grandchild who is under the
age of eighteen years and whose parent is dead, of the disponer,
or, since December 6, 2000, where the successor is a foster child,
or, under section 272 of the Finance Act 2001, where the successor is an adopted child of a natural parent.

Group B: €42,215, where the successor is, on the day the gift of inheritance is taken, a brother, a sister, or a child of a brother or sister,
of the disponer.

Group C: €21,108, where the successor, on the day the inheritance is
taken, is not entitled under class thresholds A and B above.

Groups A, B and C may be reached by a single inheritance or by a number of
inheritances spread over a number of years. All inheritances taken by a successor after December 5, 1991 (previously December 2, 1988), are aggre-
gated to determine the amount of inheritance tax payable on an inheritance
after December 2, 1998, and for the aggregation of inheritances with the
same group threshold, the base date is brought forward from December 2,
1998 to December 5, 1991.

5-15 Since December 1, 1999, inheritance tax is calculated at a standard rate and it is as follows:

TABLE 1

Portion of Value	Rate of Tax %
The threshold amount	Nil
The balance	20

Exempt and Preferred Persons and Property

5-16 Since January 29, 1985, inheritances taken by spouses and inheritances for public or charitable purposes are exempt from inheritance tax. The Capital Acquisitions Tax Act 1976, Second Schedule, Part I, paragraph 9 provides for preferential treatment of a nephew or niece of the disponer who worked with substantially on a full-time basis for a period of five years on the date of the inheritance, or assisted in the carrying on of the trade, business or profession or work of, or connected with, the office or employment of the disponer, and the inheritance consists of property which was used in connection with such trade, business, profession, office or employment, or of shares in a company owning such property;and for the purposes of computing taxation, that nephew or niece will be treated as the child of the disponer. The Finance Act 2000, section 151, introduced a new form of relief from inheritance tax in relation to certain dwellings. Section 151 provides that the inheritance of a dwelling-house taken on or after December 1, 1999, will be exempt from inheritance tax subject to the following conditions:

(1)   the beneficiary must have continuously occupied the dwelling-house as his or her only main residence for a period of three years prior to the date of inheritance;

(2)   the beneficiary must not at the date of the inheritance be entitled to any other dwelling-house or to any other interest in another dwelling-house; and

(3)   the beneficiary must continue to occupy the dwelling-house as his or her main residence for a period of six years from the date of the inheritance, except, however, where he or she is aged 55 years or more at the date of the inheritance.

Property exempted from inheritance tax includes pictures, prints, books or other items which are of national, scientific or artistic interest and which have satisfied other requirements attending such property.

Liability to Pay Tax

5-17 The successor or beneficiary has primary liability for the payment of inheritance tax due on the inheritance received by him. The personal representatives of the deceased have secondary liability for the payment of such tax, although they are primarily liable to discharge taxes owing and due under the Inland Revenue Affidavit (see Chapter 9). Section 34(3) of the Succession Act 1965 provides that the administration bond must include a provision for the payment of tax in respect of the estate of the deceased for which the personal representative is accountable and a further provision for the payment of all income tax and sur-tax payable out of the estate of the deceased (see Chapter 10).

Statutory Rights and Claims

5-18 Prior to the Succession Act 1965, a testator had unfettered testamentary freedom to dispose of his estate as he wished. He was under no legal or statutory compulsion to provide for his spouse or children in his will. The only claims on his estate were those for pre-existing debts, funeral and testamentary expenses. This continued to be the case until the enactment of the Succession Act 1965 on January 1, 1967. Since the Succession Act, a testator is still free to dispose of his property as he sees fit but the disposition of his property may be subject to adjustment by the courts if he fails, neglects or refuses to make proper provision for his spouse or children in his will; his spouse is entitled to a legal right share in his estate, and his children may apply to the court for proper provision to be made for them out of his estate. The surviving spouse may be the husband or wife of the deceased.

The Amount of the Legal Right Share

5-19 Section 109(1) of the 1965 Act provides that where a person dies wholly or partly testate leaving a spouse or children, or both spouse and children, the provisions of Part IX of the Act apply. Section 109(2) provides that references to the estate of the testator are to all estate to which he is beneficially entitled not ceasing on his death and remaining after payment of all expenses, debts and liabilities properly payable out of the estate. Section 111 goes on to provide that:

> "(1) If the testator leaves a spouse and no children, the spouse shall have a right to one-half of the estate.

(2)   If the testator leaves a spouse and children, the spouse shall have a right
to one-third of the estate."

Section 112 adds:

"The right of a spouse under section 111 (which shall be known as a legal
right) shall have priority over devises, bequests and shares on intestacy."

Thus after the payment of funeral and testamentary expenses and the discharge of all debts owing and due, the legal right of the surviving spouse
stands next in priority and must be discharged before the deceased's estate is
distributed among the beneficiaries in his will or before distribution on a partial intestacy. The claim to a legal right share arises only where the deceased
leaves a will, which either totally or partially disposes of his estate; it does
not arise on total intestacy. The legal right share of the surviving spouse is a
claim against the estate of the deceased "all or part of which may have been
left by will away from the spouse". The legal right share takes priority over
all gifts "and is particularly recognised by the provisions of s.112, which give
priority to the interest of the spouse over those created by the will".

The Nature of the Legal Right

5-20 The nature of the legal right of the surviving spouse was considered by
the Supreme Court in *Re the Estate of Cummins: O'Dwyer v. Keegan* ([1997]
2 I.L.R.M. 401). The net issue for the court to decide was whether the right
given by section 111 of the 1965 Act created an interest in the property of a
deceased testator or merely a right personal to the surviving spouse who may
elect to take such interest. Barron J. in his judgment for the court stated that
two matters were clear:

"First, the surviving spouse has a right to a share in the estate, and secondly,
this right has the same quality as an interest arising under a will or a share
arising on intestacy. The two latter interests vest on death. In my view, the
former does so also."

He cited *Re Urquhart* ([1974] I.R. 197) in support of his judgment and
referred to the judgment of Walsh J. in that case where it was stated:

"Where there is no legacy or devise or where there is a legacy or a devise
expressed to be in addition to the legal share, the legal share vests upon the
death. But when a testator in his will makes a devise or bequest to a spouse
and it is not expressed to be in addition to the share as a legal right, then the
spouse has a statutory right to take the share as a legal right - but that share
does not vest until he takes it. If the spouse does not take the share as a legal
right, then the legacy or devise under the will which vested in the spouse at

the death of the testator will remain vested in the spouse at the death of the
testator without his taking any step in relation to it. The spouse can never have
both."

The facts of the case were that Thomas Cummins and Kathleen Cummins
were husband and wife. Both of them died on the same day. At the time of the
husband's death his wife was in a coma. She died later without regaining consciousness. They had no children and both died leaving wills. The husband
made no provision for his wife in his will and his wife had not renounced her
legal right. The question arose as to whether the wife's legal right survived
her death and accordingly whether her estate should benefit by it. In applying
the construction put on section 111 of the 1965 Act by Walsh J. in *Re Urquhart* Barron J. held that:

"It must be presumed that in the absence of a renunciation under s.113 that
both spouses realised that the survivor of them would be entitled to the legal
right and, even accepting that this was an interest conditional on acceptance,
so could distribute the relevant assets as he or she wished. It is important that
the law should be certain so that those who rely upon it when they make their
wills should be in no doubt as to how their assets will be distributed not only
in expected circumstances but in unexpected circumstances also."

Accordingly, the wife's legal right share to one-half of her husband's estate
formed part of her estate on her death. Barron J. stated that:

"Even if I did not take the view as to the proper construction of the section
from the provisions to which I have referred it seems to me that the absence of
any procedure whereby the surviving spouse could be notified of the right and
given the opportunity to exercise it would have been fatal to the plaintiffs'
contentions."

The surviving spouse, it will be remembered, was in a coma.

5-21 In *Re Urquhart* a wife died leaving a will in which she bequeathed a
legacy to her husband on condition that he survived her by a month. The husband survived her by one day only. The husband died without having made
an election pursuant to section 115 of the 1965 Act. The plaintiffs claimed,
however, that the husband's legal right to one-half of his wife's estate was
property which the husband was entitled to dispose of at the time of his death.
However, as cited above, Walsh J. held that when a testator in his will makes
a devise or bequest to a spouse and it is not expressed to be in addition to the
share as a legal right, "then the spouse has a statutory right to take the share
as a legal right – but that share does not vest until he takes it." Although Barron J. in *Re the Estate of Cummins: O'Dwyer v. Keegan* cited the judgment of
Walsh J. in *Re Urquhart* as being the proper construction put on section 111,
the two cases are distinguishable by the fact that in *Re Urquhart* the surviving
spouse was given a legacy in his deceased spouse's will, but in *Cummins* the

surviving spouse was given no testamentary gift whatsoever. However, the judgment of Walsh J. was cited by Barron J. as governing circumstances similar to those in *Cummins*; therefore, where there is no gift in a will, or a gift in a will is expressed to be in addition to the legal right, the legal right share creates an interest in the estate of the deceased testator, and it seems that in all other cases a surviving spouse is merely given a personal right to elect. Kelly J. in the High Court in *Re the Estate of Cummins: O'Dwyer v. Keegan* emphasised that the legal right "has effect only in circumstances where there existed a lawful marriage between the spouses". In *Reilly v. McEntee* ([1984] I.L.R.M. 572 at 575-576) Murphy J. stated:

> "But it is not the value of this right which is in issue. It is the identity of the person by whom it is exercisable. The statute confers it on the surviving spouse and no reference has been made to any provision in the Act or any other authority which would justify the proposition that the right so conferred may be extended or transmitted to any other person."

Renunciation of the Legal Right

5-22 Section 113 of the Succession Act 1965 provides that:

> "The legal right of a spouse may be renounced in an ante-nuptial contract made in writing between the parties to an intended marriage or may be renounced in writing by the spouse after marriage and during the lifetime of the testator."

Thus a renunciation may be made not only before marriage in writing but it may also be made in writing after marriage; it may be the sole source of agreement between spouses or it may appear as a provision in a separation agreement where both spouses might mutually agree to renounce their legal rights to each other's estates. The renunciation may be a simple renouncing of rights to each other's estates or either spouse may renounce in order to benefit a child or children of the marriage. Like all transactions which require the free consent of parties, a renunciation may be set aside by the courts if it was obtained by force, fear or fraud or if the renouncing party did not have the mental capacity to appreciate the nature of a renunciation (see Appendix 4, Form No.6).

The Right of Election

5-23 The fact that the surviving spouse is given a gift in a will does not necessarily mean that the legal right share is satisfied. The gift may be worth more or less than the legal right share. However, whatever the value of the gift, section 115 of the 1965 Act presents the surviving spouse with a right of election of either taking the gift in the will or the share to which that spouse is entitled to as a legal right (see Appendix 4, Form No.3). In default of election the spouse will become entitled only to the gift in the will, and not to a share in the estate as a legal right. It may also happen that a testator may die partially intestate by acquiring more property after the execution of his will, and owing to the absence of a residuary clause in his will, an intestacy results concerning such property. (See Appendix 4 Form No.4) In such circumstances, a spouse may elect to take the legal right share, or the share under the intestacy together with any gift under the will; in default of election, the spouse will be entitled to the share under an intestacy together with the gift under the will only and will not be entitled to any legal right share. Where the surviving spouse elects in favour of the legal right share, the spouse may further elect to take any devise or bequest given to that spouse in the will which is less in value than the legal right share in partial satisfaction of that share. Section 115(4) goes on to provide that a duty is imposed on the personal representatives of the deceased testator to notify the surviving spouse in writing of the right of election in the terms of the section, which states that:

> "The right shall not be exercisable after the expiration of six months from the receipt by the spouse of such notification or one year from the first taking out of representation of the deceased's estate, whichever is the later."

The effect of section 115 was considered by the courts in *Reilly v. McEntee* ([1984] I.L.R.M. 572). In that case the testator was survived by his spouse only. A grant of letters of administration was taken out to his estate on the assumption that he had died intestate, and his spouse took possession of his property and registered herself as owner of her deceased husband's lands. The surviving spouse died without ever having known that the deceased had actually made a will. The will was discovered later under which the testator devised and bequeathed his land and all stock to his wife for life and after her death to his nephew absolutely. Murphy J. first observed that if the surviving spouse were still living, then the time period for making an election would not have run against her as she was not notified of her right of election. He said that her death gave rise to two issues:

> "First whether in all the circumstances she was or had become prior to her death entitled to the legal right as opposed to the testamentary bequest or alternatively whether the right of election survived for the benefit of the estate and accordingly was exerciseable by the plaintiff."

He decided that the surviving spouse was entitled to the testamentary benefit only as the statutory election was not made within the time prescribed. He found support for his view in the judgment of Walsh J. in *Re Urquhart* who said that:

"If the death of the spouse takes place before such election is made, then the legal share does not form part of the spouse's estate because the spouse has done nothing before death to take the share as a legal right."

Murphy J. then addressed the issue as to whether the right of election, as distinct from the property rights which the legal right might confer, passed on the death of the surviving spouse to her personal representatives. Having emphasised that it was not the value of the right which was in issue, but rather the identity of the person by whom it was exercisable, he went on to say that:

"The statute confers it on the surviving spouse and no reference has been made to any provision in the Act or any other authority which would justify the proposition that the right so conferred may be extended or transmitted to any other person."

The purpose and intent of the 1965 Act is to give the surviving spouse a personal discretion of taking either under the will or under the Act.

The Extinguishment of the Legal Right Share

5-24 The court at the time of granting a decree of judicial separation, or at any time thereafter, may make an order extinguishing the legal right share of a spouse or the share to which that spouse is entitled to on an intestacy. There is no need for the court to make any such order in the case of a decree of divorce being granted, as a spouse ceases to be a spouse from the date of the decree.

Provision for Children

5-25 Section 117(1) of the Succession Act 1965 provides that:

"Where, on application by or on behalf of a child of a testator, the court is of opinion that the testator has failed in his moral duty to make proper provision for the child in accordance with his means, whether by will or otherwise, the court may order that such provision shall be made for the child out of the estate as the court thinks just."

Ever since the enactment of the Status of Children Act 1987, the term "children" must be interpreted to include illegitimate children of a testator. The section presupposes the existence of a valid and effective will and it will form the basis of any application to the court by any child or children of the testator. Similar to the legal right share of a spouse, there must be a will in existence, but unlike the legal right share, which presents a spouse with an absolute right, section 117 only permits a child of the testator to make an application to the court to have proper provision made out of the testator's estate. However, it must first be established to the satisfaction of the court that a testator had failed in his moral duty to make proper provision for a child out of his estate.

The Moral Duty of a Testator

5-26 The time for determining the existence of a moral duty to make proper provision for a child by will is the date of death of the testator and the validity of the claim will depend on the facts existing then. However, it was considered by Blayney J. in *J. de B. v. H.E. de B.* ([1991] 2 I.R. 105 at 112-113) citing the judgment of Barron J. in *In the Goods of J.H. Deceased* ([1984] I.R. 599 at 607) that it would not be fair if the court "disregarded a relevant factor merely because it occurred after the date of death of a testator". The following criteria will be taken into account by the court when deciding whether a testator has failed in his moral duty to make proper provision for his child:

(1)   the amount left to the surviving spouse or the value of the legal right if the survivor elects to take this;

(2)   the number of the testator's children, their ages and their positions in life at the date of the testator's death;

(3)   the means of the testator;

(4)   the age of the child whose case is being considered and his or her financial position and prospects in life; and

(5)   whether the testator has already in his lifetime made proper provision for the child.

The court will assess each case on its merits and will apply objective criteria when deciding whether a moral duty exists.

5-27 The foregoing passage from the judgment of Kenny J. in *Re G.M.: F.M. v. T.A.M.* (106 I.L.T.R. 82 at 86) has been cited with approval in many later cases. In *C. and F. v. W.C. and T.C.* ([1989] I.L.R.M. 815) Finlay C.J., in his judgment for the Supreme Court, adopted and approved of the judgment of Kenny J. but added a further qualification in relation to the onus of proof which rests on an applicant in establishing the moral duty of a testator. Finlay C.J. stated that an application under section 117(1) placed "a relatively high onus of proof on an applicant" and that it is not sufficient "to establish that the provision made for a child was not as great as it might have been, or that compared with generous bequests to other children or beneficiaries in the will, it appears ungenerous". An order will not be made by the court "because it would on the facts proved have formed different testamentary dispositions". A positive failure by the testator in his moral duty must be established. Yet another criteria was introduced by Keane J. in his judgment for the Supreme Court in *E.B. v. S.S.* ([1998] 2 I.L.R.M. 141 at 150) which provides that it is:

> "not necessarily an answer to an application under s. 117 that the testator has simply treated all his or her children equally. The maxim 'equality is equity' can have no application where the testator has, by dividing his estate in that manner, disregarded the special needs (arising, for example, from physical or mental disability) of one of the children to such an extent that he could be said to have failed in his moral duty to that child. At the same time, the proper and understandable anxiety of parents to avoid any friction among their children by effecting, so far as possible, an equal distribution of their property among them must also be recognised."

By this further criterion the special needs of any particular child must also be taken into account by the court when ascertaining the moral duty of a testator to his child and may result in such a child being entitled to more of the testator's estate than the other children of the testator. Once an applicant has established that a moral duty exists the next matter to be determined by the court is what provision should be made out of the testator's estate. Yet another criterion was added to the list of matters to be taken into account by Barron J. in *McDonald v. Norris* ([1999] I.L.R.M. 270); this involved the behaviour of a child towards the testator during his lifetime.

Proper Provision

5-28 By virtue of section 117(2) the court is required to consider the application from the point of view of a prudent and just parent; it is also required to take into account the position of each of the children of the testator and any other circumstances which the court may consider of assistance in arriving at a decision that will be as fair as possible to the child or children who are applicants under section 117 and to the other children. It was said by Barron J. in *In the Goods of J.H. Deceased* ([1984] I.R. 599), citing the judgment of Costello J. in *L. v. L.*, ([1978] I.R. 288), that:

> "A parent acting prudently and justly must weigh up carefully all his moral obligations. In doing so, he may be required to make greater provision for one of his children than for others."

Therefore, the court, when considering an application by a child of a testator, must take into account all the moral duties which a testator may have had and all the claims on his resources. Adopting the approach of a prudent and just parent and taking into account the position of each of the children, the court must reach a decision which is as fair as possible to the applicant child, and where other children are concerned, to those children as well. The court must strike a balance between the children on the basis of what is just having regard to all relevant matters and to the resources of the testator. "Proper" means what is fair in the light of the matters which the court has to consider and the standard to be applied depends on the means of the testator. The power of the court under section 117 is to order such provision out of the estate of the testator as it thinks just. "Just" in the context of section 117 means "fair having regard to the interests of the applicant but also to the interests of the other children and such other person to whom the testator owed a moral duty". The power of the court arises only to remedy a failure on the part of the testator to fulfil the moral duty which he owes to his child. It is also important to remember that the moral duty of the testator to make proper provision is not confined to wills only. Section 117(1) provides that the court may intercede where a testator has failed in his moral duty to make proper provision whether by his will *or otherwise.* Kenny J. in *Re G.M.: F.M. v. T.A.M.* also referred to a lifetime provision made by a testator for his child and stated that:

> "The obligation to make proper provision may be fulfilled by will or other-wise and so gifts or settlements made during the lifetime of the testator in favour of a child or the provision of an expensive education for one child when the others have not received this may discharge the moral duty."

The Court Order

5-29 An order made by the court under section 117 will not affect the legal right share of the surviving spouse. However, where a gift is given by will to a surviving spouse, or where a spouse becomes entitled to a share in a partial intestacy, whether the gift or the share becomes part of the court's computations in determining proper provision for the child depends on the relationship of the surviving spouse to the child: if the surviving spouse is the natural parent of the child, then any gift or share on partial intestacy to that spouse will not become part of the reckoning; but where the surviving spouse happens to be a step-parent, then any such gift or share may be taken into account by the court in determining proper provision for the child.

The Time for Making the Application

5-30 Section 117(6) provides that:

> "An order under this section shall not be made except on an application made within twelve months from the first taking out of representation of the deceased's estate."

However, as a result of section 46 of the Family Law (Divorce) Act 1996 the 12-month period in section 117(6) is now amended and reduced to six months from the first taking out of representation.

Disinheriting Dispositions Made by the Deceased

5-31 Section 121 of the 1965 Act deals with dispositions which are made during the lifetime of the deceased for the purpose of disinheriting a spouse and children. The section applies to a disposition of property other than a testamentary disposition, or a disposition to a purchaser, under which the beneficial ownership of the property vests in possession in the donee within three years before the death of the person who made it, or on his death or later. On application to the court, it must be shown that the disposition was made by the deceased for the purpose of defeating or substantially diminishing the share of the disponer's spouse, whether as a legal right or on intestacy, or the intestate share of the deceased's children, or for the purpose of leaving any of the deceased's children insufficiently provided for.

Loss of Succession Rights

5-32 Not only may spouses have their statutory succession rights to the estate of the deceased extinguished following a decree of judicial separation or a decree of divorce, they may also lose their succession rights where they are convicted of certain serious criminal offences or are guilty of desertion, unless they are given subsequent gifts by the deceased in his will. Additionally, any person found guilty of an offence against the deceased, his spouse or any of his children including a child to whom the deceased stood *in loco parentis* at the time of the offence, punishable by imprisonment for a maximum period of two years or by a more severe penalty, will be precluded from taking any share as a legal right or from making an application under section 117. The latter not only envisages such offences committed by strangers against the deceased and his family but also offences committed by a spouse against the children of the deceased, offences committed by the children against the spouse, and offences committed by one child against another, thereby precluding a spouse from taking a share as a legal right and children from making applications under section 117. Since the Status of Children Act 1987, the children of the deceased will include an illegitimate child.

CHAPTER 6

The Rules of Intestacy

An Intestate

6-01 Section 3 of the Succession Act 1965 defines an intestate as "a person who leaves no will or leaves a will but leaves undisposed of some beneficial interest in his estate and intestate shall be construed accordingly". Thus, the definition of an intestate includes a person who dies totally intestate or partially intestate. Where a person dies totally intestate, the statutory rules of intestacy govern the distribution of his whole estate, while in the case of a partial intestacy, the rules of intestacy are applied only to that part of his estate which is not disposed of by his will. Notwithstanding the apparent contradiction, a person may die intestate even though he has made a will if it transpires that the will made by him is invalid. A will may be deemed invalid for a number of reasons, which have already been referred to in the earlier chapters of the book. For instance, the will may not have been properly executed in accordance with the provisions of the Succession Act, or it may cease to be the will of the testator because the contingency for which it was made failed to materialise. An intestacy may also result even though a person has left a valid will where such will was made only to give effect to a revocation clause revoking all former wills and contains no other clauses disposing of the testator's estate. Unlike wills, where the testator's estate devolves and vests in his executor, there is no person on whom the intestate's property either devolves or vests in before a grant of letters of administration is obtained. This position obviously leaves the intestate's property vulnerable and unprotected for a period of time. To remedy this, section 13 of the 1965 Act provides that the intestate's estate will vest in the President of the High Court until a grant of letters of administration is obtained, and for this purpose, the President of the High Court is to be treated as a corporation sole. However, the vesting of the intestate's estate in the President of the High Court was held not give him trustee status, nor impose any legal obligations on him – his statutory nomination is simply one of "convenience" to provide statutory cover for the intestate's estate until a grant has issued.

Succession Act Rules on Intestacy

6-02 Part VI of the Succession Act sets down the rules which govern the distribution of an intestate's estate where the intestate dies after January 1, 1967. Section 66 commences Part VI of the Act by specifying the intestate's estate that is to be made available for distribution among the beneficiaries. It provides as follows:

> "All estate to which a deceased person was beneficially entitled for an estate or interest not ceasing on his death and as to which he dies intestate after the commencement of this Act shall, after payment of all expenses, debts and liabilities and any legal right properly payable thereout, be distributed in accordance with this Part."

Thus, after the payment of such expenses as funeral, testamentary and other lawful debts owing and due by the intestate's estate, and any legal right payable out of the estate, the administrator may proceed to distribute the estate among those entitled in accordance with the rules of intestacy in the Succession Act.

Intestate Share of Surviving Spouse

6-03 A spouse's entitlement to share in the deceased spouse's intestate estate is obviously based on marital status, and while the marriage of the surviving spouse ends on the death of the other spouse, or by obtaining a valid divorce, a spouse's marital status remains unchanged where a decree of judicial separation is obtained, or where spouses agree to separate by virtue of a separation agreement. However, a spouse may also be automatically excluded from taking a share in the estate of the deceased intestate by the statutory provisions contained in Part X of the Act of 1965. Convictions for certain offences committed against the deceased will preclude a spouse from taking any share on an intestacy, for instance, convictions for the murder, attempted murder and manslaughter of the intestate, while convictions for certain less serious offences, punishable by imprisonment for a maximum period of at least two years or by a more severe penalty, preclude a spouse from claiming a legal right, although they do not preclude the spouse from taking a share on intestacy. Any share which a spouse is precluded from taking by virtue of the foregoing offences will be distributed as if that spouse had died before the deceased intestate. Where property is vested in the spouses as joint tenants, and whether one of them dies intestate or not, the right of survivorship applies, and the surviving spouse becomes entitled to the whole property, and this is so even should a spouse die leaving a will disposing of property which is subject to a joint tenancy. For the purposes of the Succession Act, "the estate or interest of a deceased person under a joint tenancy where any tenant survives the deceased person shall be deemed to be an estate or interest ceasing on his death". Where there are no complicating factors, section 67(1) of the 1965 Act provides:

> "If an intestate dies leaving a spouse and no issue, the spouse shall take the whole estate."

But section 67(2) stipulates:

> "If an intestate dies leaving a spouse and issue –
>
> (a) the spouse shall take two-thirds of the estate, and
> (b) the remainder shall be distributed among the issue in accordance with subsection (4)."

Intestate Share of Children

6-04 Section 67(3) of the 1965 Act provides:

> "If an intestate dies leaving issue and no spouse, his estate shall be distributed among the issue in accordance with subsection (4)."

Section 67(4) goes on to provide as follows:

> "If all the issue are in equal degree of relationship to the deceased the distribution shall be in equal shares among them; if they are not, it shall be *per stirpes*."

By virtue of these provisions, the children of the intestate will take equally, and remoter issue, for instance, grandchildren, will take their share *per stirpes*, where there is a child of the intestate still living. The term "issue" when used in the Succession Act, was interpreted to mean legitimate children, legitimated children and adopted children. The term excluded children to whom parents are *in loco parentis* and it was also interpreted to exclude illegitimate children by the Supreme Court. However, the Status of Children Act 1987 radically changed the law of succession for illegitimate children and they are now entitled to succeed to the intestate estates of their parents on an equal basis with other children.

The Principle of Advancement

6-05 The principle of advancement may also have to be taken into consideration when assessing the amount of the distributive share to which a child or issue of the deceased, or a child to whom the deceased was *in loco parentis*, is entitled to out of the estate. Section 63 of the 1965 Act is the relevant provision dealing with advancements. This section deals with the question of advancements made to children during the lifetime of the intestate, or during the lifetime of a testator, where such children are also given a gift in a will. For the purposes of section 63, an advancement means:

> "a gift intended to make permanent provision for a child and includes advancement by way of portion or settlement, including any life or lesser interest and including property covenanted to be paid or settled. It also includes an advance or portion for the purpose of establishing a child in a profession, vocation, trade or business, a marriage portion and payments made for the education of a child to a standard higher than that provided by the deceased for any other or others of his children."

An advancement to a child during the lifetime of the intestate will be taken into account on the distribution of the intestate's estate among his children or issue, or when ascertaining the amount of gifts given to the children of a testator in his will, subject to contrary intention expressed by the intestate during his lifetime or by the testator during his lifetime or in his will, or appearing from the circumstances of the case. For the purposes of section 63, the term "child" includes all children and a person to whom the deceased was *in loco parentis*, and, since the commencement of the Status of Children Act 1987, the illegitimate children of the deceased, or the issue of such children. The value of the advancement will be reckoned as part of the deceased's estate, and the date of valuation will be the date when the advancement was made. Thus the value of the property which the child of an intestate or testator received during the lifetime of the deceased will be treated as part of the deceased's estate for the purposes of ascertaining the amount of the child's share on intestacy or in the will, or if the child predeceases the intestate or testator, the issue of that child will become entitled to his share, after the value of the property advanced is deducted from the share. For instance, if an intestate is survived by two children leaving an estate valued at €140,000, and if it is established that during his lifetime the deceased advanced €40,000 to one of his children to set him up in business, the €40,000, in accordance with subsection (2), will be reckoned as part of the deceased's estate; thus the deceased's estate will be valued at €180,000 (€140,000 + €40,000 advanced). On distribution of his estate the two children will be entitled to €90,000 each, but taking the €40,000 advanced to one of the children into the reckoning, the distributive share of the child who received the €40,000 during the lifetime of the intestate will be €50,000, and the other child will be entitled to €130,000. The value of the advancement will remain the same as at the date of the advancement. However, if the advancement consisted of realty and not money, the child to whom it was advanced may gain an advantage over the other child if the value of realty has increased since the date it was made. For instance, if a dwellinghouse which formed the subject-matter of the advancement on a child marrying was valued at €40,000 at the date when the advancement was made, that value would remain for the purposes of calculating his share in the intestate's estate notwithstanding a substantial increase in property values at the date of death of the intestate.

6-06 But if the value of the advancement calculated at the date when it was made is equal to or greater than the share to which a child is entitled to receive under the intestacy or will, he will be excluded from the distribution of the deceased's estate. On the other hand, if the value is less than the share to which he becomes entitled, he is entitled to receive in satisfaction of his share so much more of the estate when added to the advancement as is sufficient to make up his share. The issue of a child of the deceased will be subject to the same computations. A child has also the option of retaining the advancement and abandoning his right to a share in an intestacy or under a will.

6-07 Before any advancement can be taken into account in computing the share to which a child is entitled, it must first be proved by the person asserting that an advancement was made that the child in question had actually received it, unless there is in existence some writing left by the deceased verifying this. The application of the principle of advancement is subject to a contrary intention appearing in writing or such intention being gathered from the circumstances surrounding the making of it. A contrary intention may be expressed by using the following words after the gifts to the children of the testator:

> "AND I DECLARE that no advancement within the meaning of Section 63 of the Succession Act shall be brought into account in the distribution of my estate."

Intestate Share of Parents

6-08 Section 68 of the 1965 Act provides as follows:

> "If an intestate dies leaving neither spouse nor issue, his estate shall be distributed between his parents in equal shares if both survive the intestate, but, if only one parent survives, that parent shall take the whole estate."

Under section 68 parents are entitled to an equal share in the intestate estate of their legitimate, legitimated and adopted children. The Status of Children Act 1987, since its commencement, entitles the parents of illegitimate children to succeed to the intestate estates of such children, and the restrictive provisions of the Legitimacy Act 1931 and the provisions of the Succession

Act are no longer applicable since the commencement date of that Act. However, in the case of the father of an illegitimate child, his entitlement to succeed to an intestate share is subject to an initial presumption that he has predeceased such child unless evidence in rebuttal can be provided showing that he has survived such child; if no evidence in rebuttal is provided, the mother only is entitled to the whole estate.

Intestate Shares of Brothers and Sisters

6-09 If an intestate dies leaving only brothers and sisters, his estate will be distributed in equal shares among them. Brothers and sisters are therefore entitled to their shares in the intestate's estate *per capita*. Brothers and sisters include half-brother and half-sisters, legitimated and adopted brothers and sisters, and, since the commencement of the Status of Children Act 1987, illegitimate brothers and sisters also.

Intestate Shares of Nephews and Nieces

6-10 Section 69(1) of the 1965 Act, having provided that where brothers and sisters survive the intestate only, his estate will be divided equally among them, goes on to provide that if any brother or sister does not survive the intestate, the surviving children of the deceased brother or sister will take in equal shares the share that their parent would have taken if he or she had survived the intestate, where any other brother or sister survives the intestate. Thus surviving brothers and sisters will continue to take their shares *per capita*, while surviving children of deceased brothers and sisters will take *per stirpes* the representative share of their parents. If no brother or sister survives, nephews and nieces will become entitled to equal share *per capita*, and not *per stirpes*. Where no brother or sister survives, there may be a consequent diminution of the share of certain nephews and nieces by the application again of the *per capita* rule, and the larger families of deceased brothers or sisters will benefit more than they would have done had the *per stirpes* rule been applied. Nephews and nieces of half-blood, and adopted and legitimated nephews and nieces are all equally entitled to a share in the intestate's estate.

Intestate Shares of Next-of-Kin

6-11 Section 70(1) of the 1965 Act provides that if the intestate is not survived by a spouse, issue, parents, brother, sister, or children of a brother or
sister, his estate will be distributed among his next-of-kin. In ascertaining
next-of-kin, lineal descent is preferred to collateral succession, although section 70(2) provides for an exception in the case of children of brothers and
sisters of the intestate where any other brother or sister survives him. For
instance, where the intestate is survived by a brother and the grandson of a
deceased sister, the grandson, as grandnephew of the intestate, will be entitled to the share represented by his deceased grandmother's share. However,
this is the outer extent, without involving further computations to those contained in subsection (2), to which collateral relatives will become entitled to
share in the intestate's estate, and this entitlement is further dependent on the
continued survival of a brother or sister of the intestate; where no brother or
sister survives, this collateral right to share in the intestate's estate will cease
at a point similar to where the relationship of uncle or aunt and nephew or
niece ceases. Where the intestate is not survived by any of the above relatives, his estate will be distributed in equal shares among his next-of-kin.

6-12 The ascertainment of next-of-kin is based on blood relationship to the
intestate. Section 71(1) provides that persons who are nearest in blood relationship to the deceased will take as next-of-kin. The search for a blood relative will commence with a direct lineal ancestor computed by counting
upwards from the intestate, and if he is the only survivor he takes the whole
estate. Thus, if a grandfather of the intestate is the sole survivor, he will take
the whole of the intestate's estate. However, section 71(2) provides that
degrees of blood relationship to a direct lineal ancestor are computed by
counting upwards from the intestate to that ancestor, and the degrees of blood
relationship of any other relative are ascertained by counting upwards to the
nearest common ancestor to the intestate, and then downward from that
ancestor to the relative; and if a direct lineal ancestor and any other relative
are found to be within the same degree of blood relationship to the intestate,
the other relative will be preferred to the exclusion of the lineal ancestor. If,
for argument's sake, the intestate is survived by a great-grandfather and two
aunts, the search for the next-of-kin will commence by counting upwards
from the intestate to the nearest common ancestor, *viz..* the great-grandfather;
the degrees of relationship to the intestate of the great-grandfather and the
two aunts are three degrees, and thus equal, and by applying subsection (2)
the aunts would be preferred to the great-grandfather.

Tracing Next-of-Kin

6-13 Tracing the whereabouts of the next-of-kin may prove to be a difficult task, and the assistance of persons in the business of tracing next-of-kin may be required. However, where such persons are employed, the payment for their services must not be based on a percentage of the estate which the discovered next-of-kin are entitled to receive on an intestacy; if such is the case, the method of payment may be champertous. It was said by Blayney J. in *McElroy v. Flynn and O'Flynn* (1991 I.L.R.M. 294) that such arrangements were "in the nature of champerty and void as being contrary to the policy of the law". In that case the plaintiff, who specialised in tracing next-of-kin in cases of deaths intestate, entered into an agreement with the defendants whereby he would be given a percentage of the defendants' share in the intestate estate of a deceased relative after establishing the link of next-of-kin between the defendants and the intestate. After carrying out this task the defendants informed the plaintiff that they were repudiating their agreement with him. The plaintiff sought a declaration of the court that the defendants had assigned a percentage share in the estate to him. The defendants, however, entered a counterclaim alleging that the agreement to assign a percentage share savoured of champerty and was void. The court held that the arrangement did indeed savour of champerty and was consequently void.

Partial Intestacy

6-14 Section 74 of the 1965 Act provides as follows:

> "Where the will of a testator effectively disposes of part only of his estate, the remainder shall be distributed as if he had died intestate and left no other estate."

Thus, instances of partial intestacy may arise where a testator acquires additional property after making his will and, because of the absence of a residuary clause, it remains undisposed of; or where a gift in a will lapses because a beneficiary predeceases the testator, also in the absence of a residuary clause; or where a beneficiary, after the death of the testator, disclaims a gift in the will which again contains no residuary clause. The undisposed of share must be distributed in accordance with the rules of intestacy, and the same degrees of relationship to the deceased in a total intestacy are similarly applicable in the case of a partial intestacy. Section 74 makes it clear that the undisposed of estate must be distributed as if the testator died intestate and left no other estate, thus rendering a partial intestacy independent of the provisions of any will of the deceased.

The State as Ultimate Intestate Successor

6-15 In default of the above-mentioned next-of-kin the estate of the intestate will pass to the State as "ultimate intestate successor". Section 73 of the 1965 Act replaces the old rules which dealt with the State's right of escheat and *bona vacantia* where an intestate leaves no next-of-kin. The Minister for Finance, who exercises the right to succeed on behalf of the State, is given a wide discretion by section 73 to waive the right in whole or in part and he may do this in favour of any person, and on such terms and for such money payments as he thinks proper; he may even exercise the waiver free of charge.

The Effect of Disclaiming an Intestate Share

6-16 Prior to the enactment of section 72A of the Succession Act 1965, as inserted by section 6 of the Family Law (Miscellaneous Provisions) Act 1997, some doubt existed over the entitlement to a disclaimed intestate share. The question was whether the share reverted to the estate of the deceased intestate for further distribution among the other beneficiaries, or whether the State was entitled to the share as ultimate intestate successor under section 73 of the Succession Act. Section 72A of the Succession Act as inserted by section 6 of the Family Law (Miscellaneous Provisions) Act 1997 removed all such doubt. It provides that:

> "Where the estate, part of the estate, as to which a person dies intestate is disclaimed after the passing of the Family Law (Miscellaneous Provisions) Act 1997 (otherwise than by section 73 of this Act), the estate or part, as the case may be, shall be distributed in accordance with this Part –
>
> (a) as if the person disclaiming has died immediately before the death of the intestate; and
> (b) if that person is not the spouse or a direct lineal ancestor of the intestate, as if that person had died without leaving issue."

It may be noted, however, that the section is applicable only to disclaimers made after the passing of the 1997 Act.

Loss of Intestate Succession Rights

6-17 Section 120(1) of the Succession Act 1965 provides as follows:

> "A sane person who has been guilty of the murder, attempted murder or manslaughter of another shall be precluded from taking any share in the estate of

that other, except a share arising under a will made after the act constituting the offence, and shall not be entitled to make an application under section 117."

Section 120(5) of the Act goes on to stipulate:

"Any share which a person is precluded from taking under this section shall be distributed as if that person had died before the deceased."

Therefore, by virtue of section 120(1), a person who is entitled to an intestate share but who is convicted of one of the offences mentioned will be disqualified from taking such a share. Where, for instance, the offender is the only surviving child of the intestate who has a child of his own, by virtue of section 120(5), the offender will be disqualified and his share will be distributed as if he had died before the intestate, thus allowing his child to succeed to the intestate share to which he was entitled. In such a case at least the sins of the father will not be visited on his child.

CHAPTER 7

The Personal Representatives

Executors and Administrators

7-01 Executors and administrators are also called personal representatives. They become involved immediately upon the death of the testator or intestate. Particularly so executors, who receive their appointment by will. Not so administrators, who must await their appointment by the court, although their entitlement to apply for a grant will be ascertained on the death of the deceased. Before appointment by the court, and to fill the legal lacuna, the estate of the deceased will vest in the President of the High Court by virtue of section 13 of the Succession Act 1965. As executors are personally appointed by the deceased, they may become involved in the administration of the estate on the death of the testator, although officially their entitlement to act on behalf of the estate commences from the time a grant of probate is made. Administrators will have to await the appointment of the court before they can become involved in the administration of the estate, and if any person, who is not an executor of the will or who is not an administrator appointed by the court, intermeddles with the estate, he may have the office of executor forced upon him *de son tort* (in his wrong). Once a grant has issued, the official functions of the personal representatives commence. Thereafter, they owe a duty to administer the estate in a diligent manner and they are given powers to act on behalf of the estate. The nature of their duties will depend primarily on the solvency or insolvency of the estate, and the extent of their powers will depend on the provisions of the will and the provisions of the Succession Act 1965. Once a grant has issued, the official functions of the personal representatives commence. Thereafter, they owe a duty to administer the estate in a diligent manner and they are given powers to act on behalf of the estate.

Executors

7-02 An executor is a person appointed by a testator in his will to administer his estate after a grant of probate has been obtained. Any person may be appointed by a testator to act as executor but a question may later arise whether the appointed executor is capable of acting. As a general rule, anybody who is capable of making a will is capable of acting as executor. Two executors are usually appointed. The appointment may be by will or codicil. Words of appointment similar to "I hereby appoint (*names of executors*) to be the executor of this my will" will be sufficient. It may also happen that a person may be designated in the will to carry out functions which would normally be carried out by an executor but without that person being actually appointed executor. In such a case, and in the absence of the testator appointing an executor, that person may be treated as an executor according to the tenor, and may obtain probate of the will and administer the estate of the deceased testator. An executor according to the tenor will have all the powers, functions and liabilities of an expressly appointed executor, and where a testator has expressly appointed an executor in his will, an executor according to the tenor may also join the expressly appointed executor in applying for probate of the will. In *In the Goods of Taudy* (27 L.R. Ir. 114) a direction was given in a will to discharge all debts owing by the deceased though no person was nominated as executor to pay them; as the entire estate was bequeathed to a sole and universal legatee, the court held that that person should be granted probate as executor according to the tenor. In *Re Woodroofe* (1953-1954] Ir. Jur. Rep. 36) an intended sole executor was not specifically named in the will as such but his identity was established by construing the terms of the will and the circumstances surrounding the making of it; it was held by the court that he was entitled to probate as executor according to the tenor. There is also the situation where a person may be treated as assuming the office of executor, without any formal appointment of him as executor by the testator or even knowledge of his existence by the testator, by virtue of his intermeddling or his unauthorised dealings with the estate after the death of the testator. Such a person will continue to be termed executor even though the person in whose estate he engages in unauthorised dealings died without leaving a will, a situation which would normally give rise to the appointment of an administrator. Such is known as an executor *de son tort* (in his wrong). He is one who "intermeddles" in the estate of a deceased person without appointment by will or authority of the court. If a person, by his conduct, acts as though he were an executor, the inference to be made by those with whom he deals is that he was lawfully appointed. On his part, he must have intermeddled in some way in the estate of the deceased, and a very slight form of intermeddling will suffice, even if it is for the benefit of the estate, for instance, where he carries on the deceased's business as a going concern.

Section 23(1) of the Succession Act 1965 now provides that:

> "If any person, to the defaulting of creditors or without full valuable consideration, obtains, receives or holds any part of the estate of a deceased person or effects a release of any debt or liability due to the estate of the deceased, he

shall be charged as executor in his own wrong to the extent of the estate received or coming to his hands, or the debt or liability released."

However, the subsection goes to allow the executor *de son tort* to deduct:

"(a) any debt for valuable consideration and without fraud due to him from the deceased person at the time of his death; and

(b) any payment made by him which might properly be made by a personal representative."

This provision affords some protection for an executor *de son tort* who acts bona fide in his dealings with the estate of a deceased person: it allows him to deduct any monies owing and due to him by the deceased, to make other payments which the lawfully appointed executor would have been entitled to make, and to deduct them also from the estate of the deceased.

Renunciation by an Executor

7-03 After the death of the testator, and when his will is due to be submitted for probate, an executor may accept his office by applying for probate or he may renounce it by making a formal renunciation in writing; such renunciation will accompany the papers which are required to be submitted for the taking out of a grant of probate (see Chapter 9 and Appendix 3, Form No.10). An executor's right to renounce will cease, however, after he has obtained probate of the will, because the grant of probate not only proves the will of the testator but it also confirms the executor in his office in almost priestly fashion: "once an executor, always an executor".

Administrators

7-04 An administrator is a person to whom a grant of letters of administration with the will annexed or intestate has been given by the court to administer the estate of a deceased person (see Chapters 10 and 11). He is appointed by and receives his authority from the court, unlike an executor, who is appointed by a testator and derives his authority from the will. Although the order of priority for putative administrators is that as set down by the Rules of the Superior Courts 1986, it is for the court, through the probate office or a district registry, to make grants and thus authorise administrators to act, notwithstanding any agreements which may exist between persons equally entitled to apply for a grant, or any disputes between rival claimants equally entitled to a grant. The number of administrators appointed will be limited to three unless the probate officer otherwise directs. Unlike an executor, who can always rely on the will for his appointment, an administrator is dependent upon appointment by the court; however, where there is a degree of urgency which necessitates immediate action to protect the estate of a deceased person, the court may grant an injunction, and especially so, where the application is made by a person who has prior entitlement to a grant. In *In the Goods of Cassidy* ([1904] 2 I.R. 427) the sole next-of-kin of the deceased was granted an injunction before a grant issued to restrain the deceased's landlord from interfering with his goods. After a grant has issued to an administrator, he becomes a personal representative of the estate and his position thereafter is similar in all respects to that of an executor who has been given a grant of probate. Administrators are always appointed in cases of intestacy. The priority of those entitled to grants of letters of administration intestate is set out in Order 79, rule 5 of the Rules of the Superior Courts 1986, and in the case of deaths occurring before January 1, 1967, priority is determined by the old Rules of the Superior Courts 1962. The entitlement to apply for grants of letters of administration intestate, the priority of those entitled to apply, and the documentation required for such grants is discussed at length in Chapter 10, which deals with grants of letters of administration intestate. Administrators may be appointed where a will exists in the following situations: where the testator neglects to appoint an executor; where the executor predeceases the testator; where the executor renounces his office; where the executor is incapable of performing; where the executor has failed to apply for a grant after a citation has issued; or where the executor has been passed over by the court. The form of grant such an administrator will be entitled to is a grant of letters of administration with the will annexed. The order of priority of persons entitled to apply for such grants and the documentation required to accompany such applications are discussed fully in Chapter 11.

Devolution of the Estate

7-05 The real and personal estate of a deceased person will devolve on, and become vested in, his personal representatives on his death, notwithstanding any testamentary disposition (Succession Act 1965, s.10(1)). For this purpose the personal representatives will be treated as the deceased person's heirs and assigns within the meaning of all trusts and powers (s.10(2)). The personal representatives will hold the real and personal estate of the deceased person as trustees for those entitled to it by law (s.10(3)). The real and personal estate of a deceased person will consist of all the property to which he was entitled on his death, and includes property over which he exercised by will a general power of appointment (s.10(4)). The real estate includes chattels real, and land in possession, remainder or reversion, and every estate or interest

including real estate held by way of mortgage or security, but not money arising under a trust for sale of land or money secured or charged on land
(s.4(a)); the personal estate will consist of all other forms of property. Furthermore, since the Succession Act 1965, all enactments and rules of law
concerning the administration of the personal estate of a deceased person will
apply to his real estate also as if it were personal estate: this is in furtherance
of the provisions of section 12 of the 1965 Act which assimilates the law
respecting the real and personal estate of a deceased person (s.12(1)). A grant
of representation to the deceased's estate will have equal application to both
his real and personal estate, unless there is an express limitation to the contrary (s.12(3)).

The Duties of Personal Representatives

(a) To gather in and administer the assets

7-06 Before the personal representatives can properly exercise any of their
powers under the Succession Act 1965, they must first know the extent of the
assets which comprise the estate of the deceased. The assets consist of all the
legal and equitable estate of the deceased and any estate over which he has
exercised a power of appointment by his will. These assets must first be
applied towards the discharge of debts, funeral and testamentary expenses,
liabilities and any legal right (s.45(1)).

(b) To distribute the estate

7-07 Once the personal representatives have carried out their administrative
duties, their next duty is to distribute the estate of the deceased among the
beneficiaries. For the purposes of carrying out not only administrative duties,
but also their distributive duties, the personal representatives are entitled to
sell the whole or any part of the estate (s.50(1)). By the time they come to
distribute the estate among the beneficiaries, the whole of the estate may
have already been sold by the personal representatives to discharge the payment of debts, and their distributive duties may only involve the distribution
of the remainder of the estate among the beneficiaries. Even where there are
no debts owing by the estate, the personal representatives are still entitled to
sell the deceased's estate (s.50(1)). When they decide to exercise the power
of sale the personal representatives are obliged "as far as practicable" to take
into account the wishes of beneficiaries of full age who are entitled to the
property proposed to be sold, or in the case of dispute, the majority wishes
according to the value of their combined interests (s.50(1)). It is the concern

of the personal representatives to comply with the majority wishes of the beneficiaries, and any purchaser of the property need not concern himself about whether they have acted in compliance with those wishes (s.50(1)(a)).

(c) To assent to the vesting of property

7-08   The personal representatives may transfer or assent to the vesting of land or any interest in land in the person entitled at any time after the death of the deceased testator or intestate, either subject to or free from a charge for the payment of any money which the personal representatives are liable to pay (s.52(2)). The form of assent required will depend on whether or not the land is registered. In the case of unregistered land, section 53(1) of the Succession Act specifies the form which must be used (see Appendix 4, Form No.1). The form of assent or transfer by personal representatives in the case of registered land must be in the form prescribed by section 61 of the Registration of Title Act 1964, as amended by section 54(2) of the Succession Act (see Appendix 4, Form No.2). No formalities are required to be satisfied when the personal representatives assent to the vesting of personal property.

The Power of Personal Representatives to Appropriate the Deceased's Estate

7-09   Section 55 of the Succession Act empowers the personal representatives to appropriate any part of the deceased's estate in its actual condition or state of investment at the time of the appropriation in or towards satisfaction of any share in the estate according to the respective rights of the person interested in the estate (see *H. v. O.* [1978] I.R. 194). The power to appropriate any part of the estate applies both to testate and intestate succession, although it must be exercised so as not to prejudicially affect any specific devise or bequest in a will except in cases where section 56 of the Succession Act is applicable. Unlike section 56 which gives the surviving spouse a *right* to have the dwellinghouse and household chattels appropriated in or towards the satisfaction of the legal right share (see *H. v. H.* [1978] I.R. 138), section 55 does not give other beneficiaries a *right* to have any part of the deceased's estate appropriated to them in satisfaction of any share to which they are entitled; rather, the personal representatives are given the *power* to do so (see Appendix 4, Form No.5). There are, however, certain technical requirements to be satisfied: notice of intention to exercise the power of appropriation must be served on all persons who are entitled to a share in the estate of the deceased, other than those who are not in existence at the time of the appropriation or who cannot be found or ascertained at that time after all reasonable enquiries have been carried out by the personal representatives. All persons served with this notice may within six weeks from service apply to the court to prohibit the appropriation (s.55(3)). The personal representatives must notify the surviving spouse in writing of the right conferred by section 56, and it will cease to be exercisable after the expiration of six months from such notification, or of one year from the first taking out of representation whichever is the later (s.56(5)(a)).

The Liability of Personal Representatives

7-10 Where a loss is caused to the estate owing to a breach of duty by a personal representative, he may be personally liable for what is called a *devastavit*. A *devastavit* by a personal representative renders him personally liable to both creditors and beneficiaries of the deceased. Whether there has been a breach of duty by the personal representative towards the creditors of the deceased will be determined by law, whereas a breach of duty in respect of the beneficiaries of the deceased may be determined not only by law but also by the provisions of the testator's will (see *Re Tankard* [1942] Ch. 69). The accounts kept by the personal representative may form the basis of determining his liability to creditors and beneficiaries. The accounts must record all payments of debts to creditors, and receipts for payment of same must be sought and kept by him. He will be liable for wilful default for the loss of assets gathered in by him, and his liability may be extended to include assets which he could have gathered in had he acted with due diligence (*Re Stevens* [1899] 1 Ch. 162; see *Re Gunning* [1918] 1 I.R. 221). A personal representative may also be removed from office for misconduct although the grounds for doing so must be very serious as the court considers this a drastic step and views the removal of an executor, in particular, as tantamount to overruling the wishes of the testator in the appointment of his executor (See *Dunne v. Heffernan*, unreported, Supreme Court, November 26, 1997).

devastavit

CHAPTER 8

Probate Jurisdiction

Non-Contentious Jurisdiction

8-01 Even though the High Court has full original jurisdiction over the making of grants of probate and letters of administration in both non-contentious and contentious business, the non-contentious business of the court is dealt with by the probate office or a district registry, as the case may be. An application for a grant of probate or letters of administration involving no contention may be made to the probate office or the district registry within whose district the deceased had a fixed place of abode at the time of his death. A grant of probate made by the probate office or by a district registry is known as a grant in common form; a grant of probate made by the court arising out of contentious matters is known as a grant in solemn form of law.

The Probate Office

8-02 The probate officer deals with all non-contentious matters, and where an application for a grant of probate contains no contentious matter, a grant of probate in common form will be made. The probate officer is the chief officer in the probate office and he has, what might be called, quasi-judicial powers in non-contentious probate matters.

District Probate Registry

8-03 Applications for probate or letters of administration may be made to the probate office in all cases. However, an application may be made to a district probate registry in cases where the deceased at the time of his death had a fixed place of abode within the district of the registry.

Contentious Jurisdiction

8-04 The High Court has full original jurisdiction in all probate causes and matters. The Circuit Court also has concurrent jurisdiction with the High Court to hear and determine proceedings of the following kind:

(1)   actions in respect of the grant or revocation of a grant of representation of the estate of a deceased;

(2)   proceedings in respect of the administration of the estate of a deceased person or in respect of any share therein; and

(3)   any proceedings under section 56, 115, 117, or 121 of the Succession Act 1965.

This concurrent jurisdiction of the Circuit Court is dependent, however, on the parties to the action signing a form of consent before, or at any time during, the hearing in the Circuit Court, otherwise the court will not have jurisdiction to hear the matter. Where the parties to an action in the Circuit Court do not sign a consent form, the jurisdiction of the Circuit Court will be limited as follows:

(1)   in so far as the personal estate of the deceased is concerned, the court has unlimited jurisdiction;

(2)   in so far as the real estate of the deceased is concerned, the court's jurisdiction is limited to £200 [€253.95] rateable valuation of the deceased's real estate.

Moreover, in any contentious matter arising out of an application to the probate office, and where the High Court is satisfied that the Circuit Court has jurisdiction in the matter, the High Court may remit the case to the Circuit Court where the deceased at the time of his death had a place of abode, and that court will proceed as if the application had been made to it in the first instance. In any probate matter which appears doubtful to a district probate registrar whether a grant should be made or not, or where any question arises in relation to a grant, the district probate registrar is under a statutory duty to send a statement of the cause or matter in doubt to the probate office in order to seek the directions of the High Court. The High Court may direct the district probate registrar to process the application for a grant, or may forbid any further processing of the grant, allowing the person seeking a grant to apply to the High Court, or if the case is within the jurisdiction of the Circuit Court, by applying to that court.

The Nature of the Grant

8-05 The nature of the grant made by the probate office or district registry will depend on whether or not there is a will, and also whether the will appoints executors who may apply for a grant. Where there is a will and there are executors appointed by it, they may apply for a grant of probate. However, where a will appoints no executors, those persons who are entitled to apply first in the order of priority set down in Order 79, rule 5, of the Rules of the Superior Courts 1986 may apply for a grant of letters of administration with the will annexed. Where there is an intestacy, persons who are first entitled to apply in the order of priority set down in Order 79, rule 5, may apply for a grant of letters of administration intestate. The correct documentation must also accompany the application for the relevant grant. A second grant may also be necessary if the sole surviving personal representative dies during the course of the administration of the estate; in such an event, the persons entitled to apply in the order of priority for the original grant will be entitled to apply for a grant of letters of administration with the will annexed *de bonis non*, and the same applies where a grant *de bonis non* is required to complete the administration of an intestate estate.

The Probate of a Will

8-06 After a will has been submitted to probate, a copy of it will be issued by the probate office under the seal of the High Court, accompanied by a certificate signed by the probate officer stating that the original will has been duly proved and registered and that administration has been granted to the applicant (see Appendix 3, Form No. 5). At least 14 days must elapse from the death of the testator before a grant of probate can issue, unless otherwise ordered by the court or the probate officer. Besides granting administration of the estate, it also authenticates the will and is evidence of the character of the executor; the seal of the High Court will be judicially noticed in any proceedings where it is adduced as evidence in the course of a trial. Before a court can grant any relief based on a will, it must first be established that the will was admitted to probate. A grant of probate, once made, is conclusive until it is revoked, and it cannot be questioned in any other court.

CHAPTER 9

A Grant of Probate

Entitlement to Apply for a Grant

9-01 Only persons who are appointed executors by a testator in his will are entitled to apply for a grant of probate, or persons who are constituted executors according to the tenor by virtue of the functions assigned to them by the will.

The Necessary Documentation

9-02 When applying for a grant of probate the following documents must be lodged in the probate office or a district probate registry, as the case may be:

(1) an application for a grant;

(2) the original will and codicils (if any);

(3) a copy or engrossment of the will;

(4) the oath of the executor;

(5) an Inland Revenue affidavit (including Probate Tax Return Form where relevant);

(6) an affidavit of due execution of the will and codicils (if any);

(7) special affidavits where necessary;

(8) the death certificate of the testator.

The most important of these documents are considered below.

The Original Will

9-03 Every will, or copy of a will, exhibited in the oath of the executor or in the oath of the administrator for grants with the will annexed must be marked by the executor or administrator and by the person before whom it is sworn. So as not to interfere with the will or the attestation of it, any such marking is usually made on the back of the will. Copies of wills must be written in a legible hand, or printed, typewritten or photocopied, subject to the directions of the probate officer. If no attestation clause appears in a will submitted for probate or letters of administration with the will annexed, or if the attestation clause is insufficient, an affidavit from at least one of the attesting witnesses will be required confirming that the provisions of the Succession Act regarding the execution of wills have been complied with, and a note signed by the probate officer will be made on the copy of the will to the effect that such an affidavit has been filed (see Appendix 3, Form No. 1). If it transpires that both attesting witnesses are dead or, for some other reason, no affidavit can be obtained from either of them, other persons who were present at the execution of the will may instead make an affidavit deposing to the facts surrounding the execution of the will. Where interlineations or other alterations appear on the face of the will, affidavit evidence may be required to show that they appeared on the will before its execution, unless such interlineations or alterations were themselves duly executed by the testator and attesting witnesses, or were recited in or identified by the attestation clause. Any codicils to the will of the testator will be treated in like fashion when they are submitted for probate as testamentary instruments. Where it is reasonable to believe that a person made a will or other testamentary instrument and it is not produced, any application for its production must be by way of court order and sought by means of a motion grounded on affidavit evidence whether or not a suit is pending. Or alternatively, if it can be shown that a will or other testamentary instrument is in the possession, power or under the control of a definite person, a *subpoena* may be issued for its production by the probate officer instead of incurring the expense of seeking a court order. Copies of wills or other testamentary instruments must be bespoken in the probate office, and every such copy must be certified by the probate officer.

The Oath of Executor

9-04 The oath of the executor must be subscribed and sworn as an affidavit and filed in the probate office (see Appendix 3, Form No. 2). Every will or copy of a will exhibited in the oath of the executor must be marked by him and by the person before whom the oath is sworn, and any such marking must be made on the back of the will so as to distinguish it from the will itself and the attestation clause. The oath must contain the following information:

(a) The correct name and address of the executor

9-05 The oath may be used as an amending document to correct a misspelled version of the executor's name in the will, for instance, if the executor's name is John Whyte and he is named John White in the will. It may also be required to elaborate on a description given in the will; for instance, the testator may appoint "my wife" as executrix, and if that is the case, the oath should state that the executrix is the lawful wife of the deceased testator.

(b) The name, address and description of the deceased testator

9-06 Where the deceased used an alias for the purposes of his will, his correct name and alias must be stated in the oath. However, where an alias was used for a particular reason, for instance, for the purposes of acquiring property which is now part of his estate, the alias should be added to his correct name. The address and description of the deceased must appear also, and if the deceased lived at a different address from that mentioned in the will, the oath should show that he formerly lived at the address stated in the will. Where a foreign address of the testator appears in the will, a statement should be included in the oath to the effect that the deceased died domiciled in Ireland. The description of the deceased testator must be included and, strictly speaking, if he changed his occupation since the date of the will, this must be referred to in the oath of the executor.

(c) The date of death of the testator

9-07 The precise date of death must be stated in the oath. However, the date of death appearing in the oath is not *prima facie* evidence of the death of the deceased. A duly authenticated death certificate must be produced to provide evidence of death. The place of death should also be included in the oath. Where the deceased died on board a ship on the high seas, the name of the ship should be stated together with the fact that he died and was buried at sea, and if such were the case, the same being duly authenticated by the ship's records. However, where the testator is known to have died but the precise date of his death is unascertainable, the oath should state when the deceased was last seen alive and when and where the body was discovered.

(d) The relationship (if any) between the executor and testator

9-08 The relationship between the executor and the deceased testator, if one exists, must appear in the oath. If the relationship is inconsistent with that stated in the will, the correct relationship should appear in the oath. In the case of children, where the relationship is other than legitimate, the nature of the relationship should be stated: legitimated and adopted children should be stated as such, and in the case of illegitimate children, they should be described as the natural son or daughter of the testator.

(e) "That he did not intermarry with any other person after the making of the will"(see Appendix 3, Form No. 2)

9-09 The main reason for including this statement in the oath is that if the testator had married after the making of his will, that subsequent marriage would have revoked his will, unless it was established that his will was made in contemplation of that marriage. Any doubt on the matter may have to be resolved by an application to the court (see Chapter 4).

(f) The gross value of the testator's estate

9-10 The oath must contain a statement of gross value of the estate of the testator without any deductions for debts (see Appendix 3, Form No. 2). This gross value appearing in the oath should be the same as the statement of gross value in the Inland Revenue Affidavit.

(g) Renunciation by one of the executors

9-11 Where there are two executors appointed by the will and one of them wishes to renounce his office, he must sign a renunciation form and this must be referred to and exhibited in the oath by the remaining executor who is applying for the grant of probate (see Appendix 3, Form No. 10). An executor who renounces his right to probate will cease to be an executor and his right of representation for the estate of the testator will devolve as if that person had not been appointed executor by the testator.

(h) Affidavits of due execution and special affidavits

9-12 Where it appears from the will that there is no attestation clause or that the attestation clause in the will fails to satisfy the statutory provisions for due execution contained in the Succession Act 1965, an affidavit of due execution becomes necessary (see Appendix 3, Form No.1).

The Death Certificate

9-13 Every application for a grant of probate must include the death certificate of the deceased testator among the documents required for obtaining a grant of probate. In the absence of a death certificate, other evidence which tends towards proving that the testator was buried may be acceptable in place of a death certificate; for instance, a photograph of a headstone or tombstone or the production of mortuary cards may be sufficient. Where there is no death certificate or sufficient alternative evidence of death, an order may have to be sought of the court presuming the death of the testator. For the court to presume the death of a testator, it must first be established that seven years have elapsed since the testator was last heard of. It must further be established that the testator was not last heard of for seven years by persons who might reasonably be expected to have heard from him.

The Inland Revenue Affidavit

9-14 Before an application for a grant of probate can be made, an Inland Revenue Affidavit must be prepared by the executor setting out the particulars and assets of the estate of the deceased testator. Section 38 of the Capital Acquisitions Tax Act 1976 begins by providing that the Inland Revenue Affidavit has the meaning assigned to it by the Finance Act 1894. The section then goes on to specify the type of particulars of the deceased testator's estate which must be disclosed in the affidavit.

9-15 The probate office or district probate registrar must deliver to the Revenue Commissioners, in the case of probate or letters of administration with a will annexed, the Inland Revenue Affidavit and a copy of the will, if required to do so.

9-16 On receipt of the Inland Revenue Affidavit, the Revenue Commissioners must be satisfied that an adequate payment on account of inheritance tax in respect of the property passing under the testator's will, or Part IX of the Succession Act 1965, or section 56 of the Succession Act 1965, has been made, or that the payment of inheritance tax can be deferred for the time being without serious risk of such tax not being recovered. A certificate will then be issued that the Inland Revenue Affidavit was delivered to them and that payment has been made or that it has been deferred. However, a certificate may be withheld where the Revenue Commissioners believe that that payment of tax cannot be deferred without serious risk of tax not being recovered.

Probate Tax

9-17 Although probate tax was abolished by the Finance Act 2001, section 225, it is still chargeable in respect of deaths occurring before December 6, 2000. The Finance Act 1993 introduced this form of tax. Returns for payment of this tax where chargeable must be prepared and submitted to the Revenue Commissioners at the same time as the Inland Revenue Affidavit. The taxable value of the testator's estate is subject to a two per cent probate tax. A probate tax return must be made even though the estate of the testator is not liable to such tax. The executor is primarily liable to submit a probate tax return with secondary liability vesting in the beneficiaries. Liability for probate tax arises when the taxable value of the testator's estate exceeds the €12,697.38 threshold, which is index-linked and which is based on the gross value of the estate as stated in the Inland Revenue Affidavit.

9-18 In the case of a surviving spouse taking an absolute interest in property, the probate tax liability on the property is abated to nil. Where the surviving spouse takes a limited interest in property, the probate tax liability on the property is postponed until the death of that spouse. For instance, where the spouse is given a life interest in the property, probate tax is postponed until the death of the spouse, and it becomes payable nine months after that date. Where the taxable value of the property is less than the index-linked €12,697.38 threshold, there is no probate tax liability. Marginal relief is further provided by the proviso that the amount of tax payable cannot exceed the excess over the threshold of €12,697.38. For instance, if taxable value of the estate is €12,887.84, the probate tax payable is the excess of the value over the threshold of €12,697.38; the tax payable will be €190.46, and not two per cent of the taxable value of €12,887.84, which otherwise increases the tax payable to €384.73.

A *De Bonis Non* Grant

9-19 Where, in the course of administering the estate of the deceased, the executor dies, a grant of letters of administration with the will annexed *de bonis* will have to be sought to continue with the administration, and the person entitled to apply for such grant is the person next entitled in the order of priority as set out in Order 79, rule 5(6), of the Rules of the Superior Courts 1986. The documentation which is required to apply for a grant of letters of administration with the will annexed must accompany the application for a grant *de bonis non* (see Appendix 3, Form No. 8).

A Grant of Letters of Administration with the Will

The Nature of the Grant

10-01 Grants of letters of administration with the will annexed, like grants of probate, are based on the existence of a will, and the reason why such a grant, rather than probate, is made is because the will fails to appoint an executor, or the appointment of the executor fails by death or renunciation, or as a result of a citation, the executor has been cleared off or has been otherwise removed. Such grants also share a common feature with grants of letters of administration intestate, besides both being grants of letters of administration, in that the persons entitled to apply for both types of such grants are set out in the Rules of the Superior Courts. However, the order of priority of persons entitled to apply for grants of letters of administration with the will annexed is based on the will, while the order of priority of the persons entitled to apply for letters of administration intestate will be based on the statutory rules of intestacy. As in the case of applying for grants of probate, where there is no contention involved in applying for grants of letters of administration with the will annexed, the probate officer, or a district probate registrar, within whose district the deceased had a fixed place of abode at the time of his death, may make such a grant.

Persons Entitled to Apply for a Grant

10-02 Where a grant of letters of administration with the will annexed is sought, Order 79 of the Rules of the Superior Courts 1986 sets out an order of priority of those persons entitled to apply for such a grant as follows:

(1)   the residuary legatee or devisee holding in trust for other persons;

(2)   the residuary legatee or devisee with a life interest;

(3)   any other residuary legatee or devisee or the personal representative of any residuary legatee or devisee;

(4)   any residuary legatee or devisee for life jointly with any ultimate residuary legatee or devisee on the renunciation or consent of the remaining residuary legatees or devisees for life;

(5)   where the residue is not in terms wholly disposed of, the probate officer may, if he is of opinion that the testator has nevertheless disposed of the whole or substantially the whole of the estate as ascertained at the time of the application for a grant, allow a grant to be made to any legatee or devisee entitled to, or to share in, the estate so disposed of, without regard to the person entitled to share in any residue not disposed of by the will;

(6)   where the residue is not wholly disposed of by the will, any person (other than a creditor) entitled to a grant in the event of a total intestacy, according to the order priority set out in sub-rules (1) to (5) of Order 79; and

(7)   any legatee or devisee or any creditor or the personal representative of any such person.

A grant will not be made to more than three joint applicants unless the probate officer otherwise directs. Where the person entitled to a grant in the order of priority above assigns his beneficial interest in the will to another person the assignee will take his place in the order of priority in applying for a grant. Rule 5(7) of Order 79 provides that where a gift in a will fails because it was witnessed by the beneficiary, or the spouse of a beneficiary, such beneficiary will not be entitled to apply for a grant as a beneficiary in the will. Rule 5(9)(a) provides that a grant may be given to any person who is entitled to it without notice to other persons entitled in the same class, unless the probate officer requires notice to the be given. In relation to the class itself, a grant will be given to a living member of that class in preference to the personal representative of a member of that class who has died following the death of the testator.

The Necessary Documentation

10-03 In applying for a grant of letters of administration with the will annexed, all documents which are required to be submitted with the application for the grant are similar to those required to be submitted in applying for a grant of probate, with the exception of the executor's oath. In the case of letters of administration with the will annexed, the executor's oath is replaced by the administrator's oath. An important additional document known as the administration bond is also required to be submitted.

The Administrator's Oath

10-04 The administrator's oath must take the form of an affidavit and must be filed in the Probate Office or in the appropriate district registry. The form of affidavit is that as prescribed by the Rules of the Superior Courts (see Appendix 3, Form No. 4). The will itself, or a copy of the will, must be exhibited and marked by the administrator and by the person before whom the oath is sworn, and where a mark is required to be made on a will, it must be made in such a way as to be clearly distinguishable from the will and the attestation clause; a mark appearing on the back of a will shall be sufficient.

The Administration Bond

10-05 Section 34 of the Succession Act 1965 provides that every person who applies for a grant of administration must enter into a bond to inure for the benefit of the President of the High Court, and if the High Court, the probate officer, or the district registrar so requires, with one or more sureties conditioned for collecting, getting in, and administering the estate of the deceased. The administration bond must be in a penalty of double the amount at which the estate of the deceased is sworn, unless the court, probate officer or district probate registrar directs it to be reduced. It may also be directed that more than one administration bond be given so as to limit the liability of any surety to such amount as the court, probate officer or district probate registrar thinks reasonable. The administration bond will be in such form as the President of the High Court may prescribe. Where the condition of an administration bond has been broken, the High Court may order that the bond be assigned, and the person to whom the bond is assigned will be entitled to sue in his own name, and to recover as though he were a trustee for all persons interested the full amount recoverable in respect of the breach of the condition of the bond. The current form is set out in Appendix Q, Part II of the 1986 Rules (see Appendix 3, Form No. 16).

A *De Bonis Non* Grant with the Will Annexed

10-06 Where a grant of letters of administration with the will annexed has been made and the estate is in the course of administration, but, owing to the death or incapacity of the administrator, the administration is unable to proceed, an application may be made by the person next entitled in order of priority under Order 79, rule 5(6); such a person will be entitled to apply for a grant of letters of administration with the will annexed *de bonis non*, thus allowing that person as the new administrator to continue with the administration of the estate. The same documents that were required to be submitted for the first grant must also be sent with the documentation required for the *de bonis non* grant (see Appendix 3, Form No.8).

CHAPTER 11

A Grant of Letters of Administration Intestate

Persons Entitled to Apply for a Grant

11-01 As stated in Chapter 6, which deals with the rules of intestacy, an intestacy results when a person dies without making a will, or where the will made by him is invalid owing to the presence of a vitiating element. The rules of intestacy ascertain the persons who are entitled to share in the intestate's estate and the rules of court determine who is entitled to apply for a grant of letters of administration. The current rules are found in the Rules of the Superior Courts 1986. Rule 5(1) provides that in determining the order of priority of persons entitled to apply for letters of administration to estates of persons who died on or after January 1, 1967 (the enactment date of the Succession Act), wholly intestate and domiciled in Ireland, the persons having a beneficial interest in the estate will be entitled to apply for a grant in the following order:

(1) The surviving spouse.

(2) The surviving spouse jointly with a child of the deceased nominated by the surviving spouse. The obvious advantage to be derived here is that if the surviving spouse is elderly, assistance in the administration may be required and a child may be nominated for this purpose, and it also dispenses with the need for further grants should the death of the surviving spouse occur during the course of the administration.

(3) The child or children of the deceased.

(4) The issue of any child who has died during the lifetime of the deceased.

(5) The father or mother of the deceased intestate.

(6) The brothers and sisters of the deceased whether of the whole or half-blood.

(7) Where any brother or sister survived the intestate, the children of a predeceased brother or sister.

(8) The nephews and nieces of the intestate (whether of the whole or half-blood).

(9)   The grandparents of the intestate.

(10)   The uncles or aunts (whether of the whole or half-blood) of the intestate.

(11)   The great-grandparents of the intestate.

(12)   Other next-of-kin of the nearest degree (whether of the whole or half-blood) preferring collaterals to direct lineal ancestors.

(13)   The nominee of the State.

(14)   Rule 5(2) provides that the executor or administrator of any of the above persons, excluding the personal representative of the nominee of the State, will have the same entitlement to a grant as the person whom he represents, save only that a grant will be made to a living member of a class entitled to a grant in preference to the executor or administrator of a member of that class who has died after the intestate, unless the court or probate officer otherwise directs. The reason for this apparently is that live interests are preferred to dead interests.

(15)   Rule 5(3) provides that where there are conflicting claims for a grant among the class entitled to apply, it will be made to such of the claimants as the probate officer may select, having given not less than 21 days' notice to all rival claimants, and if any objection is made to the probate officer's selection within that period, the court may make the selection. Suitability and best interests of the estate will be the criteria where rival claimants are equally determined to apply for a grant.

(16)   Rule 5(4) provides that if all of the persons entitled to apply for a grant have been cleared off, a grant may be made to a creditor of the deceased, or to the executor or administrator of a creditor. A citation to accept or refuse administration may be used by a creditor to clear off persons with a prior entitlement, and in the event of persons cited failing to apply for a grant, the creditor may himself apply for a grant.

(17)   Rule 5(5) provides that the Adoption Acts 1952-1988 (as construed in accordance with section 27(3) of the Status of Children Act 1987) will apply in determining the title to apply for a grant as they apply to the devolution of an estate on intestacy. On production of the necessary affidavit exhibiting the birth certificate and adoption order for the purposes of establishing relationship to the intestate, a grant will issue.

Rule 5(1) provides that in determining the order of priority of persons entitled to apply for letters of administration to estates of persons who died on or after January 1, 1967 (the enactment date of the Succession Act) wholly intestate and domiciled in Ireland, the persons having a beneficial interest in the estate will be entitled to apply. Rule 5(3) provides that where there are conflicting claims for a grant among the class entitled to apply, it will be made to such of the claimants as the probate officer may select, having given not less than 21 days' notice to all rival claimants. Rule 5(4) provides that if all of the persons entitled to apply for a grant have been cleared off, a grant may be made to a creditor of the deceased, or to the executor or administrator of a creditor.

11-02 Before the coming into force of the Status of Children Act 1987, illegitimate children were totally excluded from succeeding to the intestate estate of their father, and had only limited rights of intestate succession to their mother's estate. Section 9 of the Legitimacy Act 1931 provided that where the mother of an illegitimate child died intestate and is not survived by legitimate issue, the illegitimate child, or if he has died, his issue, will be entitled to any interest in her estate as if he had been born legitimate. Since the Status of Children Act 1987 the definition for the purposes of the Succession Act 1965 was extended to include illegitimate children, thus giving them equal entitlement to apply for a grant together with the other children of the intestate under Order 79, rule 5(1)(c).

11-03 The provision in the Succession Act which provides that relatives of the half-blood shall be treated as, and shall succeed equally with, relatives of the whole blood in the same degree is reflected in the order of priority of those persons entitled to apply for a grant in Order 79, rule 5(1), of the Rules of the Superior Courts 1986. There is also a provision in the 1965 Act which deals with the ascertainment of the next-of-kin and provides that collateral relatives are preferred to direct lineal ancestors and this provision is also taken into account regarding the order of priority in applying for grants by Order 79, rule 5(1).

11-04 The range of persons entitled to apply for a grant under Order 79, rule 5, is extended to include the personal representatives of the deceased persons who were entitled to apply for a grant in the absence of any member of the class to which the deceased persons belonged still living and entitled to apply unless the court or probate officer otherwise directs.

11-05 Order 79, rule 5, is expressly stated to be applicable to cases of total intestacy only. In cases involving partial intestacies, the same rules of intestacy will be used in distributing that part of the deceased estate which is not disposed of by his will. In such cases, the executor who has probate, or an administrator who has letters of administration with the will annexed, will continue the administration of the estate without being required to obtain a separate grant for the partial intestacy.

The Necessary Documentation

11-06 The documents required to be lodged in the probate office or a district registry are the same as those required to be lodged for the purposes of applying for a grant of letters of administration with the will annexed, with the obvious exception of a will. The administrator's oath must contain information relevant to an application for letters of administration intestate, including the priority of the person applying for the grant, or the way by which he has acquired priority by clearing off persons entitled before him.

A *De Bonis Non* Grant Intestate

11-07 In the event of the administrator dying during the course of administration, a further grant will be required to complete the administration. The person who is next entitled in the order of priority, when the application for the original grant was made, may continue with the administration of the deceased's estate after applying for a grant of letters of administration intestate *de bonis non*. Any additional documentation will be read together with the documentation already on record for the original grant (see Appendix 3, Form No.9).

CHAPTER 12

Caveats and Citations

12-01 The primary reason for entering a caveat is that the caveator will be informed of any applications for grants of probate or letters of administration in relation to the estate of the deceased, and in order to give him time to prepare a challenge to the making of any such grant. A citation, on the other hand, is usually entered by a citor in the probate office because of the tardiness of the executor or administrator in applying for a grant. Caveats and citations therefore may be used for opposing the issuing of a grant or for compelling a person with prior title to apply for a grant.

Caveats

12-02 A caveat may be used to prevent the making of a grant of probate or letters of administration without notice to the person entering the caveat. No grant can issue until the caveat is removed or ceases to have effect. However, where a caveat is warned by the person on whom it is served, the caveator is obliged "either to abandon his claim to a grant or to take contentious proceedings in furtherance of his claim". The caveat must be lodged in the probate office or a district registry (see Appendix 3, Forms No.12 and No.13). The procedure in relation to the issuing of caveats is set out in Order 79, rules 41-51, of the Rules of the Superior Courts and is as follows:

(1)   The caveat must be lodged in the probate office or a district registry.

(2)   It must be dated on the day in which it is lodged and it remains in force for six months and will cease to have effect after that time unless it is renewed.

(3)   It must contain the name and address of the caveator and the registered place of business of the solicitors lodging the same, or if it is lodged personally, the name and address within the jurisdiction of the person lodging it.

(4)   If it is shown that a person knowingly lodges a caveat in the name of a fictitious person or gives a false address of a person on whose behalf it purports to be lodged in the probate office, the same will be viewed as a contempt of court.

(5)   Upon lodgement of the caveat in the probate office, the probate officer will immediately send notice of its lodgement to the district registry in which it is alleged the deceased resided at the time of his death, or in which he is known to have had a fixed place of abode at the time of his death.

(6)   If, coincidentally, the caveat is lodged on the same day on which a grant is made or on the day on which notice of its lodgement in the probate office is sent to a district registry, the grant will remain unaffected.

(7)   The response to a caveat is a warning which must be filed in the probate office and it must be served by delivery of a copy at the place mentioned in the caveat as the registered place of business of the caveator's solicitors, or at the address for service of the person who lodged the caveat, within 14 days of its date of issue; otherwise the warning will be deemed inoperative unless otherwise ordered by the Court or the probate officer.

(8)   The probate officer will also send a copy of the warning signed by him to the solicitors or person at their registered place of business or at the address of service mentioned in the warning and will keep a record of such posting.

(9)   The warning must contain the name and address of the person on whose behalf it is issued, and if such person claims under a will, the date of the will and the registered place of business of the solicitors lodging the warning, or if there is no professional representation, the address for service within the jurisdiction.

(10)   The caveator must then enter an appearance in the probate office within 14 days of the service of the warning, although time for the appearance may be extended until an action in default of appearance is taken.

(11)   Where no appearance has been entered, in order to clear off the caveat, an affidavit of service of the warning and a certificate of non-appearance must be filed in the probate office unless the Court or probate officer makes a special order to the contrary.

12-03 A caveat may:

(1)   be lodged in order to give the caveator time to make enquiries and to obtain information to determine whether there are grounds for opposing a grant.

(2)   be lodged in order to give the caveator an opportunity to raise any question arising in respect of the grant on motion before the court.

(3)   be used as a preliminary step to the commencement of an action between the caveator and the person warning the caveat – the warning and the appearance disclosing the respective interests of the parties.

Citations

12-04 Although the High Court may summon any person named as executor in a will to prove or renounce probate, the probate office, functioning as the non-contentious wing of the High Court in probate matters, may issue a citation under the seal of the High Court and signed by the probate officer. It recites on its face that a cause or matter is before the court, states the interest of the citor in the estate of the deceased testator or intestate, orders the party cited to enter an appearance, and to carry out such functions as are stated in its form of issue (see Appendix 3, Form No.15). The procedure in relation to the issuing of citations is set out in Order 79, rules 52-58 of the Rules of the Superior Courts and is as follows:

(1)   Before a citation issues from the probate office under the seal of the High Court, an affidavit must be filed in verification of the facts outlined on its face. Only the probate office may issue citations.

(2)   The citation itself will be served on the person cited if he resides within the jurisdiction or, if he resides abroad, is an Irish citizen. Where the person to be served resides abroad and is not an Irish citizen, notice only of the citation will be served on him. The affidavit for a citation to be served out of jurisdiction must state whether or not the person to be served is an Irish citizen. The citation itself, or notice of it, must be served personally where possible. Where a personal service of the citation is intended, it is unnecessary to seek an order of the court regarding service. In the event of personal service not being possible, the citor must apply to the court for directions as to the mode of service.

(3)   A citation will not be signed by the probate officer until the citor enters a caveat against any grant being made in respect of the estate of the deceased to which the citation relates, and notice of the same must be sent to the district registry of the dis-

trict in which the deceased appears to have resided at the time of his death.

(4)   A citation must be written, typed or printed and a copy must be made by the citor or his solicitors and must be taken to the probate office. It must be signed and sealed and a copy deposited in the probate office. The citation must contain the address of the registered place of business of the solicitors extracting the citation, or, if extracted personally, an address for service within the jurisdiction.

(5)   The person served with the citation is allowed 14 days to enter an appearance but the time for entering an appearance will be extended until such time as an action in default shall be taken under rule 57 of Order 79.

(6)   If no appearance is entered to the citation duly served on a person to accept or refuse probate or administration within the time prescribed by rule 56, or within the time for appearance as extended by the court or the probate officer, his non-appearance will be taken as a renunciation of his right to apply for probate or letters of administration, and the citor will then be entitled to obtain a side-bar order from the probate officer to that effect.

(7)   If the person cited to accept or refuse probate or letters of administration indicates that he intends to apply for a grant on entering his appearance, the citor will be entitled to obtain a side-bar order from the probate officer to that effect. However, where a citation is extracted citing a person with prior title to apply for a grant to accept or refuse probate or letters of administration, any failure by him to enter an appearance will be taken as a renunciation of his prior title to apply for a grant. The citor himself may then apply for a grant himself in place of the person cited. The citor's entitlement to apply for a grant is derived from the cited person's failure to enter an appearance and may not be based on kinship or otherwise to the deceased. A citation may be used, for instance, to cite the person entitled to accept or refuse administration (Appendix 3, Form No.15).

12-05 If there was no procedure for issuing citations, the administration of estates could be suspended for intolerable lengths of time, or, indeed, could continue to remain unadministered. An executor or person entitled to apply for a grant is under no compulsion of law to apply for a grant, as there is no legal obligation to apply for a grant or liability for a failure or refusal to do so. Although a citation, like a caveat, may be used as a first step to test the validity of a will, once probate of the will has been granted in common form, citation or caveat procedures are no longer the appropriate procedures to adopt for the commencement of an action to prove a will in solemn form: this will require a probate action by the interested parties.

Appendix 1

Specimen Instruction Sheet

Full Name and Address of Testator ....

Occupation ....

Any Former Will? Yes/No Where held ....

Full Name and Address of Executor(s) ....

Testator's Family: ....
Wife's/Husband's Full Name ....
Children's Full Names and Ages ....
Next-of-kin (where relevant) ....

Particulars of Testator's Assets ....

Reasons for excluding spouse and/or children ....

Renunciation by Spouse? ....

Spouse as Universal Legatee and Devisee (proviso of one month survival)
Yes/No ....
Spouse Sole Executor Yes/No ....

Specific Devises and Bequests ....
Dwellinghouse and premises ....
Household chattels ....
Personal effects ....
Special articles (*e.g.* a painting) ....
Investments ....
Pecuniary legacies ....
Charitable legacies ....
Residue ....
Settlement of Residue on Children's Income at age 18/21/25 ....

Capital at age 18/21/25 ....
If Trust intended, Powers of Trustees: ....
to invest ....
to advance ....
to lend ....
to apportion...
to appropriate...
to manage land...
to run business as going concern ....
Section 63 Succession Act not to apply ....
Payment for Professional Work by Executor/Trustee ....

Original Will to be held by ....

Costs ....

Date...

Place (if not solicitor's office) ....

Signed by the testator ....

Witnessed (by two) ....

Appendix 2

Specimen Wills

While specimen wills may be useful guidelines in the preparation of wills of testators coming from different backgrounds, it is important to remember that "no will has a twin brother" and the will must be designed to suit the testator's wishes, and not to suit a convenient specimen.

1. Husband's (or Wife's) Will Leaving All Property to Spouse with Substitutional Provisions for Children

I (name of testator/ testatrix) of (address) make this as and for my last will and testament and hereby revoke all former wills and testamentary dispositions heretofore made by me.

1.   If my wife/husband (name) survives me by thirty days I give devise and bequeath the whole of my estate to him/her and appoint him/her my executor/executrix. If my wife/husband does not survive me by thirty days the following provisions shall apply:

2.   I Appoint AB of (address) and CD of (address) (hereinafter called "my Trustees") to be executors and trustees and appoint them trustees for the purposes of the Settled Land Acts 1882 to 1890, Conveyancing Acts 1881 and 1911, and Section 57 of the Succession Act 1965.

3.   I Appoint my Trustees guardians of my infant children.

4.   I give devise and bequeath to my Trustees the whole of my estate upon trust to sell the same (with power to postpone such sale in whole or in part for such time or times as they shall think fit) and to hold the same or the proceeds of sale thereof on the following trusts:

   (a)   To pay my debts, funeral and testamentary expenses;

   (b)   (Provision for legacies, house and/or contents to, etc., if intended)

   (c)   To divide the residue (hereinafter called "my Residuary Estate") among such of my children as shall survive me and reach the age of 18 (or 21) years and, if more than one, in equal shares absolutely BUT if any child of mine dies before me or before attaining a vested interest leaving a child or children then such shall on reaching the age of 18 years take *per stirpes* the share his/her or their parent would otherwise have taken, and if more than one, in equal shares absolutely AND I DECLARE that no advancement within the meaning of Section 63 of the Succession Act 1965 shall be brought into account in the distribution of my estate;

(d)   To pay to each child on reaching the age of 18 years the annual income of his or her share of my Residuary Estate until he or she reaches the age of 21 years.

5.   In addition to all statutory powers which my Trustees may have, they shall have the following powers:

(1)   To exercise the power of appropriation under Section 55 of the Succession Act 1965 without serving any of the notices or obtaining any of the required consents.

(2)   To buy any asset of my residuary estate.

(3)   To apply for the benefit of any beneficiary under the age of 18 (or 21) years as my Trustees think fit the whole or any part of the capital of my Residuary Estate to which that beneficiary is entitled or may in future be entitled and on becoming absolutely entitled he shall bring into account any payments received under this clause.

(4)   To invest and change investments freely as if they were absolute owners beneficially entitled and to invest in unsecured interest free loans or other non income-producing assets including property for occupation or use by any beneficiary.

6.   All income received after my death shall be treated as income of my estate regardless of the period to which it relates and the statutory rules concerning apportionment and the rules in *Howe v. Dartmouth* and *Allhusen v. Whittell* shall not be applied.

7.   Any of my Trustees who is engaged in a profession shall be entitled to be paid fees for work done by him or his firm on the same basis as if he were not one of my trustees but employed to act on behalf of my Trustees.

8.   I Declare that no Trustee of this my Will shall be liable for any loss not attributable to the Trustees own dishonesty or to the wilful commission by the Trustees of any act known to be a breach of trust.

In Witness whereof I have hereunto signed my name the day and year first above written.

SIGNED PUBLISHED AND DECLARED by the said   as and for his last Will and Testament in the presence of us who at his request and in his presence and in the presence of each other (all three being present at the same time) have hereunto subscribed our names as witnesses.

2. Husband's (or Wife's) Will Leaving All Property to Spouse for Life with Gifts Over

I (name of testator/testatrix) of (address) make this as and for my last will and testament and hereby revoke all former wills and testamentary dispositions heretofore made by me.

1.   I appoint AB of (address) and CD of (address) (hereinafter referred to as "my Trustees") to be the executors and trustees of this my will and appoint them trustees for the purposes of the Settled Land Acts 1882 to 1890, Conveyancing Acts 1881 and 1911, and Section 57 of the Succession Act 1965 and in the event of my wife's/husband's death I also appoint them guardians of my infant children.

2.   My Trustees shall hold the whole of my estate upon trust either to retain or sell it on the following trusts:

(a)   To pay my debts, funeral and testamentary expenses;

(b)   To pay the income from the residue to my spouse during his/her lifetime and after his/her death to divide the residue equally among those of my children who survive me and reach the age of 18 (or 21) years but if any child of mine dies before me or before attaining a vested interest leaving children then those children shall on reaching the age of 18 years take equally the share which their parent would otherwise have taken AND I DECLARE that no advancement within the meaning of Section 63 of the Succession Act 1965 shall be brought into account in the distribution of my estate;

(c)   To pay to each child on reaching the age of 18 years the annual income of his or her share of my estate until he or she reaches the age of 21 years.

3.   In addition to all statutory powers which my Trustees may have they shall have the following powers:

(1)   To exercise the power of appropriation under Section 55 of the Succession Act 1965 without serving any of the notices or obtaining any of the required consents;

(2)   To buy any asset of my estate;

(3)   To apply for the benefit of any beneficiary under the age of 18 (or 21) years as my Trustees think fit the whole or any part of the capital of my estate to which that beneficiary is entitled or may in future be enti-

tled and on becoming absolutely entitled he shall bring into account any payments received under this clause;

(4)   To invest and change investments freely as if they were beneficially entitled and to invest in unsecured interest free loans or other non income-producing assets including property for occupation or use by a beneficiary.

4.   All income received after my death shall be treated as income of my estate regardless of the period to which it relates and the statutory rules concerning apportinment and the rules in *Howe v. Dartmouth* and *All-husen v. Whittel* shall not be applied.

5.   Any of my Trustees who is engaged in a profession shall be entitled to be paid fees for work done by him or his firm on the same basis as if he were not one of my Trustees but employed to act on the behalf of my Trustees.

6.   I declare that no Trustee of this my Will shall be liable for any loss not attributable to the Trustees own dishonesty or to the willful commission by the Trustee of any act known to be a breach of trust.

In witness whereof I have hereunto signed by name the   day of   20 .

SIGNED by the Testator in our presence and signed by us in the presence of him/her and of each other.

3.   Unmarried Person's Will with Legacies to Nephews and Residue to Sister

I (name of testator/testatrix) of (address) make this as and for my last will and testament and hereby revoke all former wills and testamentary dispositions heretofore made by me.

1.   I appoint AB of (address) and CD of (address) to be the executors and trustees of this my last will (hereinafter called "my trustees") and I direct my trustees to discharge all my just debts, funeral and testamentary expenses.

2.   I appoint my trustees to be trustees for the purposes of the Settled Land Acts 1882 to 1890 and for the purposes of Section 57 of the Succession Act 1965 and for the purposes of the Conveyancing Acts 1881 and 1911 and I DECLARE that a sole Trustee for the time being hereof and of every Trust Fund hereby created shall be competent to act for all the purposes of the said Acts and this my Will including the receipt of Capital monies under the Settled Land Acts.

3.   To the Secretary for the time being of the   Society (Charity) having its principal offices at (address) I GIVE AND BEQUEATH the sum of €5,000.00 (Five Thousand Euro) for the charitable purposes in Ireland of the said Society.

4.   To my nephew No. 1   (name) of   (address) I GIVE AND BEQUEATH the sum of €5,000.00 (Five Thousand Euro).

5.   I GIVE AND BEQUEATH to my Trustees the sum of €200,000.00 (Two Hundred Thousand Euro) to be held by them in trust for my nephew No. 2 (name) of (address) and I DIRECT that if my said nephew shall be under the age of 21 years (or 18 years) at the date of my death my Trustees shall be empowered to apply in addition to the income from the said legacy or any investment representing the same the entire of the capital representing the said legacy for the purposes of the maintenance, benefit, advancement, and in particular the education of my said nephew in such manner and at such times as they in absolute discretion shall think fit and any payments made by my Trustees may be made by them to my nephew's Guardian or to any other person in whose custody or charge my said nephew may be without my Trustees being responsible for seeing to the actual application thereof and upon my said nephew attaining the age of 21 years (or 18 years) the said legacy and the investments representing the same and any accumulated income thereof shall be paid and transferred to him but if my said nephew shall die under the age of 21 years (or 18 years) the said legacy and investments and accumulated income therefrom shall revert to and become part of my residuary estate.

6.   Any monies requiring investment hereunder may be laid out in or upon the acquisition of security of any property of whatsoever nature and wheresoever situate including in particular but without prejudice to the generality of the foregoing words stocks, shares or securities of any kind whatsoever, insurance policies of any description and any house or flat or apartment as a residence for any beneficiary hereunder to the intent that my Trustees shall have the same full and unrestricted powers of investing in all respects as if they were absolutely entitled thereto beneficially and subject to no restriction with regard to advice or otherwise in relation to investment.

7.   As to all the rest residue and remainder of my estate whatsoever and wheresoever situate I GIVE DEVISE AND BEQUEATH same to my sister (name) of (address) for her own use and benefit absolutely. If my said sister predeceases me then in that event I GIVE DEVISE AND BEQUEATH all the rest residue and remainder of my Estate to my brother (name) of (address) for his own use and benefit absolutely.

IN WITNESS whereof I hereunto set my hand this the   day of 20 .

SIGNED PUBLISHED AND DECLARED by the said testator as and for his last Will and Testament in the presence of us both present at the same time who at his request in his presence and in the presence of each other have hereunto subscribed our names as witnesses.

Appendix 3

Probate Forms

See Appendix Q of the Rules of the Superior Courts 1986
(S.I. No. 15 of 1986)

No. 1

AFFIDAVIT OF ATTESTING WITNESS.

In the estate of   late of   deceased.

I,   of   aged   years and upwards, make oath and say that I am one of the subscribing witnesses to the last will [*or* codicil] of the said   late of [*address and description*] deceased; the said will [*or* codicil] bearing date the   day of   20   , and that the said testator executed the said will [*or* codicil] on the day of the date thereof, by signing his name [*or* affixing his mark, being illiterate *or* unable to write from physical debility], at the foot or end thereof as the same now appears thereon, in the presence of me and of   the other subscribed witness thereto, both of us being present at the same time – and we thereupon attested and subscribed the said will [*or* codicil] in the presence of the said testator and of each other. [*if will was signed with a mark add*:] And I further say, that before said testator executed said will [*or* codicil] in manner aforesaid, same was truly, audibly, and distinctly read over to him by me, and said testator appeared fully to understand the same, and was at the time of the execution thereof of sound mind, memory, and understanding.

Sworn, &c.

Note: The will should not be marked by the deponent or by the commissioner.

No. 2

OATH OF EXECUTOR.

In the estate of   late of   deceased.

I,   of   aged   years and upwards, make oath and say, that I believe the paper writing hereto annexed, and marked by me, to contain the true and original last will [*or* last will with   codicils]   of   late of [*address and description*] deceased; that same was made by the said after attaining the age of   years, and that he did not intermarry with any person after the making of same; that I am the [*state relationship*] of the said   and the sole executor in the said will [*or* will and codicils] named [*or as the case may be*]; that I will faithfully administer the estate of the said testator, by paying his just debts and the legacies bequeathed by his said will [*or* will and codicils], so far as the same shall thereto extend and the law bind me; that I will exhibit a true inventory of the said estate, and render a true account thereof, whenever required by law so to do; that the testator died at   on the   day of   [*where application is made in District Probate Registry add*] and that the testator has at the time of his death a fixed place of abode at   within the district of   and that the whole of the estate which devolves on and vests in his legal personal representative amounts in value to [*the gross assets, without any deductions for debts*] and no more, to the best of my knowledge, information and belief.

Sworn, &c.

No. 3

OATH OF ADMINISTRATOR WITH THE WILL.

In the estate of   late of   deceased.

I,   of   aged   years and upwards, make oath and say,
that I believe the paper writing hereunto annexed, and marked by me, to contain the true and original last will [or last will with   codicils] of
late of [address and description], deceased, and that same was made by the
said   after attaining the age of   years, and that he did not intermarry with any person after the making of same, and   that
the executor therein named, predeceased the said testator [or as the case may
be], and that I am the [state relationship] of said testator and the residuary
legatee named in the said will [or as the case may be], that I will well and
faithfully administer the estate of the said testator, by paying his just debts
and the legacies bequeathed by his said will [or will and codicils] and distributing the residue of his estate according to law; and that I will exhibit a true
and perfect inventory of the said estate, and render a true account thereof
whenever required by law so to do; and that the testator died at   on
the   day of   [where application is made in a District Probate
Registry, add: and had at the time of his death a fixed place of abode at
.   within the district of   ] and that the whole of the personal
estate of the said testator amounts in value to the sum of [the gross personal
estate, without any deductions for debts] and that the whole of the real estate
of the said testator which devolves on and vests in his legal personal representative is of the market value of [the amount shown in the affidavit of market value] and no more to the best of my knowledge, information and belief.

Sworn, &c.

No. 4

OATH OF ADMINISTRATOR.

In the estate of   late of   deceased.

I,   of   aged   years and upwards, make oath and say that late of [*address and description*], deceased, died intestate [*state here whether bachelor, &c., and clear off all other parties entitled to grant in priority to applicant; and state capacity in which applicant seeks administration*]   that I am the lawful   of said deceased and that I will well and faithfully administer the estate of the said deceased by paying his just debts and distributing the residue of said estate according to law, and that I will exhibit a true inventory of the said estate and render a true account thereof, whenever required by law so to do; that the said deceased died at on the   day of   [*where application is made in a District Probate Registry, add:* and that the said deceased had at the time of his death a fixed place of abode at   within the district of   ] and that the whole of the personal estate of the said deceased amounts in value to the sum of [*the gross personal estate without any deductions for debts*] and that the whole of the real estate of the said deceased which devolves on and vests in his legal personal representatives is of the market value of [*the amount shown in the affidavit of market value*] and no more to the best of my knowledge, information and belief.

    Sworn, &c.

No. 5

PROBATE.

Be it known, that on the   day of   the last will, a copy of which, signed by the Probate Officer [*or* District Probate Registrar] is hereunto annexed, of   deceased, who died on or about the   day of [*where grant issued out of a District Probate Registry, insert* and who at the time of his death had a fixed place of abode at   within the district of] was proved, and registered in the Probate Office [*or* District Probate Registry] and that the administration of all the estate which devolves on and vests in the personal representative of the said deceased was granted by the Court to   named in the said will [and codicils] he having been first sworn faithfully to administer the same.

[*Insert appropriate certificate as to Inland Revenue affidavit*].

No. 6

ADMINISTRATION INTESTATE.

Be it known that on the   day of   letters of administration
of the estate which devolves on and vests in the personal representative of
deceased, who died intestate on or about   the   day of   [*where
grant issued out of a District Probate Registry, insert* and who at the time of
his death had a fixed place of abode   at   within the district of
] were granted by the Court to   he having been first sworn faithfully
to administer the same.

[*Insert appropriate certificate as to Inland Revenue affidavit*].

No. 7

ADMINISTRATION WITH THE WILL ANNEXED.

Be it known, that   deceased, who died on or about the   day
of   at   [*where grant issued out of a District Probate Registry, insert* and who at the time of his death had a fixed place of abode   at
within the district of   ] made and duly executed his last will (and
codicils) a copy of which, signed by the Probate Officer [*or* District Probate
Registrar] is hereunto annexed and did therein name [*or* did not therein name
any] executor [*or as the case may be*].
     And be it further known that on the   day of   letters of admin-
istration with the said will annexed of the estate which devolves on and vests
in the personal representative of the said deceased were granted by the Court
to   he having previously been sworn faithfully to administer the
same, according to the tenor of the said will (and codicils).

[*Insert appropriate certificate as to Inland Revenue affidavit*].

No. 8

ADMINISTRATION WITH THE WILL ANNEXED (DE BONIS NON).

Be it known that   deceased, who died on or about the   day of
        20   , at   [*where application is made in District Probate
Registry, add* and who at the time of his death had a fixed place of abode at
within the district of   ], made and duly executed the last will [a copy
of which, signed by the Probate Officer [*or* District Probate Registrar], is
hereunto annexed] and did therein   name   executor, and that on
the   day of   [probate of the said will and administration of the estate
which devolves on and vests in the personal representative] of said deceased
were granted at the Probate Office [*or* District Probate Registry aforesaid] to
[which   now remains of record in   ] who after taking such
        upon   intermeddled in the estate of said deceased; and afterwards
died on the   day of   20   , leaving part thereof unadministered, and that
on the   day of   20   , letters of administration of the said estate which
devolves on and vests in the personal representative of the said deceased and
which was so left unadministered, with said will annexed, were granted at the
Probate Office [*or* District Probate Registry] to   he having been
first sworn faithfully to administer the same.

   [*Insert appropriate certificate as to Inland Revenue affidavit*].

No. 9

ADMINISTRATION INTESTATE (DE BONIS NON).

Be it known, that   deceased, died intestate on or about the
day of   20   , at   [*where application is made in District
Probate Registry, add* and at the time of his death had a fixed place of abode
at   within the district of   ], and that since   death,
on the   day of   , letters of administration of the estate which
devolves on and vests in the personal representative of the said deceased
were granted at the Probate Office [*or* District Probate Registry] to
[which letters of administration now remain of record in   ] which said
after taking such administration upon   intermeddled in the estate of
said deceased; and afterwards, on or about the   day of   20   ,
died   leaving part thereof unadministered, and that on the
day of   20   , letters of administration of the said estate which
devolves on and vests in the personal representative of the said deceased and
which was so left unadministered were granted to   he having been
first sworn faithfully to administer the same.

[*Insert appropriate certificate as to Inland Revenue affidavit*].

No. 10

RENUNCIATION OF PROBATE OR ADMINISTRATION WITH THE WILL ANNEXED.

In the estate of   Whereas

late of   late of

                                        deceased, died on the   day

            deceased.   of   19   , at

[*where application is made in a District Probate Registry, add* having at the time of his death a fixed place of abode at   within the district of   ] and whereas, he made and duly executed his last will [*or* will and   codicils] bearing date the   day of   20   , and thereof appointed   executor [*or as the case may be*].

Now I, the said   aged   years and upwards, do declare that I have not intermeddled with the estate of the said deceased, and will not hereafter intermeddle therein, with the intent to defraud creditors, and I do hereby expressly renounce my right to probate of the said will [*or* will and codicils], [*or* to letters of administration with the said will [*or* will and codicils] annexed] of the estate of the said deceased.

            Dated

            (Signed)

Witness

No. 11

RENUNCIATION OF ADMINISTRATION.

In the estate of   Whereas

late of   late of   deceased

died a   and intestate

deceased.   on

the   day of   20   , at [*where application is made to a District Probate Registry, add*   having at the time of his death a fixed place of abode at   within the district of   ].

And whereas, I   of   am his [*state relationship*].

Now I, the said   aged   years and upwards, do hereby renounce all my right to letters of administration of the estate of the said deceased.

Dated

(Signed)

Witness

No. 12

CAVEAT.

Let nothing be done in the estate of *A.B.*, late of   deceased, who died on the   day of   at   unknown to me [*E.F.* being the solicitor of] *C.D.*, of   in the County of   having interest.

[Signed) *E.F.*

[*Registered place of business*].

or C.D.,

[*Address for service*].

No. 13

Warning to Caveat.

To *C.D.* [*or E.F.*, solicitor of *C.D.*]

You are hereby warned within fourteen days after the service of this warning upon you, inclusive of the day of such service, to enter an appearance [for *C.D.*], in the Probate Office, to the caveat entered by you in the estate   of late of   , deceased, who died at   on the   day of 20   , and set forth your [*or* your said client's] interest, and take notice, that in default of your so doing, the said caveat will cease to have any effect.

(Signed)

Probate Officer.

Issued at the instance of *R.S.* [*here set forth what interest R.S. has and if under a will or codicil, set forth the date thereof, if any, and give an address for service.*]

[*Indorsement to be made after service.*]

This warning was served by *J.K.* on   at [*here state where and how the service was effected*] on the   day of   20   .

(Signed) *J.K.*

No. 14

Appearance to a Warning or Citation (Except one to Accept or Refuse).

In the estate of *A.B.*, deceased, late ofl, *C.D.*, [*or E.F.*] appear [for *C.D.*.], being the brother, and one of the next-of-kin of the said *A.B.*, deceased

[*or any other interest the said C.D. may have*].

Dated

(Signed) *E.F.*, solicitor for *C.D.*

[*Registered place of business*].

or C.D. [*address for service*].

No. 15

CITATION TO ACCEPT OR REFUSE ADMINISTRATION.

To   of

Whereas, it appears by an affidavit of   of   filed in the Probate Office on the   day of   20   , that you are the lawful [*widow, child, or as the case is*] and only next-of-kin of the   said deceased, intestate, who died on or about the   day of   20 , and that [*party issuing citation*] claims to be [*state interest as creditor, next-of-kin (giving relationship), &c.*].

NOW THIS IS TO COMMAND YOU, that within fourteen days after service hereof on you, inclusive of the day of such service, you appear in the Probate Office, personally, or by your solicitor, and accept or refuse letters of administration of the estate of the said deceased, as of a person dying intestate, otherwise to show cause, if any, why the same should not be granted or committed unto the said

Dated

(Signed)

                                        Probate Officer.

        Solicitor for said

    [*Registered place of business*].

Form No. 16

ADMINISTRATION BOND

The High Court

The Probate Office/The District Probate Registry at

We

        are each liable in full to pay to the President of the High Court the sum
of   for which payment we bind ourselves and each of us and
our

Sealed with our seal(s) and dated the   day of   20 . The
condition of this obligation is that if the above-named

the

of

deceased, and the intended administrator/administratix of the estate of the
said deceased,

do, when lawfully called on in that behalf, make or cause to be made a true
inventory of the said estate which has or shall come into his/her hands, possession or knowledge, or into the hands, possession or control of any other
person for him/her;

do exhibit the said inventory or cause it to be exhibited in the Probate Office
(or in the district probate registry at   ) whenever required by law to
do so;

do well and truly administer the said estate according to law, paying all the
debts owed by the deceased at the time of his death, all death duties payable
in respect of the estate of the deceased for which the personal representative
is accountable and all income tax and surtax payable out of the estate,

distributing all shares in the estate to those entitled by law thereto and as the
law requires him/her;

and further, do make or cause to be made a true account of the said administration whenever required by law to do so;

and further do, if so required, render and deliver up the letters of adminis-tra-tion in the High Court if it shall hereafter appear that any will was made by the deceased which is exhibited in the said Court with a request that it be allowed and approved accordingly;

then this obligation shall be void and no effect, but shall otherwise remain in full force and effect.

Signed, Sealed and Delivered
    by the within-named

in the presence of

Appendix 4

Succession Act Forms

Specimens of Assents and Notices

Form No. 1

ASSENT BY PERSONAL REPRESENTATIVES TO UNREGISTERED LAND

We,   (names of personal representatives) the personal representatives of   (name of deceased) late of   (address of deceased) deceased hereby assent to the vesting in   (name of beneficiary) of ALL THAT AND THOSE the land and premises situate at   (state where) for all the estate and interest of the aforesaid   (deceased's name) therein at the time of his death.

In witness whereof we have hereunto set our hands this   day of   20 .

This form is sufficient to assent and convey the interest to which the beneficiary is entitled to in the will and it may be registered in the Registry of Deeds. This form may be extended to include other matters like, for example, a reference to the will of the deceased and the grant of probate made in relation to it. However, the above specimen will be sufficient to satisfy the provisions of Section 53 of the Succession Act.

Form No. 2

ASSENT BY PERSONAL REPRESENTATIVES TO REGISTERED LAND

An assent by the personal representatives to registered land must be done in accordance with section 61 of the Registration of Title Act 1964 and in the form required by the Land Registration Rules 1972. There is no discretion as regards the form the documents should take in assenting to registered land; they must be drafted in compliance with the rules and forms prescribed by the 1972 Rules.

Notice by personal representatives of the right of election to a spouse

Such a notice must be sent by the personal representatives in pursuance of section 115 of the Succession Act where the deceased leaves a will or where he dies leaving a will but also partially intestate.

Form No. 3

FORM OF NOTICE (WHERE THE WILL DISPOSES OF
ALL THE DECEASED'S PROPERTY)

In the Estate of   (name of deceased) Deceased

1.   We,   (names of personal representatives), being the personal representatives of the aforesaid deceased late of (address of deceased) who died on the   day of   20 hereby give notice to you being the surviving spouse of the aforesaid deceased in pursuance of section 115 of the Succession Act 1965.

2.   Under and by virtue of his will dated the   day of   20   the aforesaid deceased devised and bequeathed in clause of his will attached hereto.

3.   You are hereby notified that you may elect to take the devise and bequest given to you in clause of the will attached hereto or your legal right share in pursuance of Section 111 of the said Act as the said devise and bequest was expressed not to be in addition to the said legal right share.

4.   You are hereby further notified that in default of election by you to take either the said devise or bequest in the will attached hereto or the said legal right share that you shall become entitled only to take the said devise and bequest in the will.

5.   This right of election given to you in pursuance of Section 115 of the said Act shall not be exercisable by you after the expiration of six months from the date of receipt hereof or one year from the   day of 20_, it being the date when the grant of probate of the deceased's will was first made to us whichever is the later.

Dated the   day of   20 .

Signed (by the personal representatives)

Form No. 4

FORM OF NOTICE (WHERE THE DECEASED LEAVES A WILL AND
IS PARTIALLY INTESTATE)

In the Estate of   (name of deceased) Deceased

1.   We,   (names of personal representatives), being the personal representatives of the aforesaid deceased late of   (address of deceased) who died on the   day of   20   hereby give notice to you being the surviving spouse of the aforesaid deceased in pursuance of section 115 of the Succession Act 1965.

2.   Under and by virtue of his will dated the   day of   20   the aforesaid deceased devised and bequeathed in clause of his will attached hereto.

3.   The aforesaid deceased died intestate in respect of the following property:

       (The property and value thereof subject to the intestacy should be stated here and the share the surviving spouse is entitled to depending on whether or not there are children surviving)

4.   You are entitled as spouse to elect to take under and by virtue of the provisions of Section 115 of the Succession Act 1965 either:

       (i)   Your Legal Right Share under the Act; or

       (ii)   Your Intestate Share in respect of the property not disposed of by the deceased in his will and the devise and bequest given to you in his will.

5.   In default of electing between (i) and (ii) of paragraph 4 above you will be entitled only to your intestate share in respect of the property not disposed of by the deceased in his will and the devise and bequest given to you in his will.

6.   This right of election given to you in pursuance of Section 115 of the said Act shall not be exercisable by you after the expiration of six months from the date of receipt hereof or one year from the   day of   20_   it being the date when the grant of probate of the deceased's will was first made to us whichever is the later.

Dated the   day of   20 .

Signed (by the personal representatives)

Form No. 5

FORM OF NOTICE FOR RIGHT OF APPROPRIATION OF
DWELLING AND HOUSEHOLD CHATTELS

In the Estate of   (name of deceased) Deceased

1.   We,   (names of personal representatives) being the personal
representatives of the aforementioned deceased late of   (address of
deceased) who died on the   day of   20   hereby give you notice
being the surviving spouse of the aforementioned deceased pursuant to
section 56 of the Succession Act 1965 that you are entitled to require
us to appropriate to you the dwelling in which you were ordinarily res-
ident at the time of the death of the deceased and also any household
chattels in or towards satisfaction of any share of the estate to which
you are entitled in pursuance of Section 55 of the said Act.

2.   The right of appropriation given to you by Section 56 of the said Act
may also be exercised by you in relation to the share of any infant for
whom you are trustee under Section 57 of the said Act or otherwise if
your aforesaid share is insufficient to enable the aforesaid appropriation to be made.

3.   Further take notice that if you fail neglect or refuse to exercise the
aforesaid right of appropriation after the expiration of six months from
the receipt of the notice hereof or one year from the   day of   20_
being the date of the grant of probate of the deceased's will first made
to us the aforesaid right shall not be exercisable thereafter.

4.   Confirmation of your intention to exercise the aforesaid right must be
notified to us in writing before the expiration of the aforesaid dates.

Dated and Signed (by the personal representatives)

Form No. 6

SUCCESSION ACT 1965
RENUNCIATION OF RIGHTS

PART IX

TO ALL WHOM IT MAY CONCERN

I,   (name of spouse renouncing) of   (address of spouse) wife/husband of   (name of other spouse) of same address hereby revoke all and any rights or claims to which I may be or may become entitled to any share or interest in the estate of the said   (name of spouse) under and by virtue of the provisions of the Succession Act 1965, and particularly under and by virtue of Part IX of the said Act on the death of the said   (name of other spouse) and I hereby declare that the nature and extent of the said rights referred to above have been explained to me prior to the execution of this Renunciation and I am aware of and understand the nature and effect of this Renunciation and have executed this Renunciation for good and sufficient reasons.

Dated the   day of   20   .

Signed by the said   (name of spouse renouncing)

in the presence of   (name of witness)

Index

References are to paragraph number.

ademption, 5-04
  application of, 5-04
  gift of money, 5-04
  specific company shares and, 5-04
  specific devises and, 5-04
  specific legacies and, 5-04
administration bond, 10-05, App.3,
  form no.16
administrators, 7-01 *et seq, see also*
  executors
  appointment of, 7-01, 7-04
  appropriation of deceased's estate
    by, 7-09
  devastavit by, 7-10
  devolution of estate to, 7-05
  duties of, 7-02
    assent to vesting of property,
      7-08
    to administer assets, 7-06
    to distribute the estate, 7-07
    to gather assets, 7-06
  grant of letters of administration to,
    7-04
  intestacy and, 7-904
  liability of, 7-10
  number of, 7-04
  oath of, 10-04, App 3-3, App 3-4
  powers of, 7-01
  priority of, 7-04
advancement, 6-05-6-07
  during lifetime of intestate, 6-05
  during lifetime of testator, 6-05
  meaning of, 6-05
  principle of, 6-05, 6-07
  retention of, 6-07
  value of, 6-05, 6-06
annuity, 5-02
attestation clause, 1-03, 2-06, 2-08,
  2-09, 2-11, 9-03, 9-04, 9-12,
  10-04

beneficiary,
  application for grant of probate by,
    1-09
  children. *see* children
  dissatisfaction of, 1-09
  duty of care of solicitor to, 2-14
  gift lacking, 5-04
  income of, 5-08
  inheritance tax and, 5-01, 5-10,
    5-12, 5-15, 5-16
  knowledge and approval of will,
    2-10
  legal right share, 5-18 *et seq*
  marriage of to witness, 2-08
  predecease testator, 2-15
  predeceased is child, 5-05
  relationship of with testator, 5-01,
    5-04, 5-05
  specific legacy and, 5-08
  testamentary gifts, failure of, due
    to, 5-03, 5-06
  witness as, prohibition of, 2-08,
    3-05
bequest, 1-02, 5-01, 5-02, *see also*
  devise, gift, legacy *and* **testa-**
  mentary gifts
  interest, accrual of on, 5-09
  interpretation of, 5-09
  legal right share and, 5-18, 5-19,
    5-21
  purpose of, 5-09
capacity to make will, 3-01 *et seq,*
  see also **will**
  age of testator, 3-01
  elderly testator, 1-04
  evaluation of by court, 2-10
  fraud, 3-07
  mental condition of testator, 3-01
  mental ill-health, 3-05
  presumption of, 2-10
  revocation and, 4-07

capacity to make will — *contd.*
  sound disposing mind of testator,
    1-04, 3-01, 3-04
  undue influence, 1-04, 3-06, 3-07
capital acquisitions tax, 5-10
caveats, 12-01 *et seq*
  caveators,
    enter appearance of, 12-02
    name and address of, 12-02
    obligations of, 12-02
  date of, 12-02
  form, App 3-12
  lodgment of, 12-02, 12-03
  procedure for, 12-02
  reason for entering, 12-01
  response to
  warning to, 12-02, App 3-14
Circuit Court,
  jurisdiction of, 8-04
codicils, 2-10, 2, 11, 2-12, 2-13, 9-02,
  9-03
  due execution of, 2-12, 2-13
  purposes of, 2-13
  revival and, 2-13, 4-16, 4-18
  revocation and, 2-13, 4-14
  signatures and, 2-13
  use of, 2-13
champerty, 6-13
child/children
  adopted, 5-13, 6-04
  advancement and, *see* **advance-**
    ment
  brother, of, 5-13
  child, meaning of, 6-05
  court order under s.117 for, 5-27
  dependent, 1-02
  foster, 5-13
  grandchild, 5-13, 6-04
  illegitimate, 5-23, 6-04
  interest on gift to, 5-09
  intestate share of, 6-04
  issue, interpretation of, 6-04
  legal right share of, 5-18
    renunciation of, 5-20
  legitimate, 6-04
  moral duty to, 5-23-5-25
  per stirpes, 6-04
  predeceased beneficiary of, 5-09

child/children — *contd.*
  provision for, 5-17, 5-23-5-26
  rights of, 1-01, 5.17, 5.18
  sister, of, 5-13
  taxation, computation of, for, 5-15
  testator of, gifts to, 5-09
  time to make application to court
    for, 5-28
  trustees for, 5-09, *see also* **trustees**
  under age of majority, 1-02
citations, 12-01, 12-04, App.3, form
  no.14, App.3, form no.15
construction of will, *see also* **will**
  form of will, 1-02
  instruction sheet, 1-01, App.1
  instructions for making will, 1-01
court, *see also* **Circuit Court** *and*
  High Court
  administrators, appointment of by,
    see **aministrators**
  capacity to make will and, 2-10,
    see also **capacity to make a**
    will
  caveats, 12-03
  citations and, 12-04
  contempt of, 12-02
  directions of, 11-04, 12-02
  improperly attested wills before,
    2-07
  interpretation of word presence by,
    2-06
  letters of administration and, 11-01
  omnia praesumuntur rite et solem-
    niter esse acta,
    application of by, 2-09
  rules of, 11-01
  testator's signature in question
    before, 2-09
District Probate Registry, 1-05,
  8-03, *see also* **probate**
destruction of will, 4-02, 4-05, 4-06,
  4-08, 4-15, *see also* **will**
devise, 1-02, 5-01, 5-02, 5-04, 5-07,
  5-18, 5-19, 5-21, 7-09, 10-02,
  see also **bequest, gift, legacy,**
  real estate *and* **specific legacy**
  ademption and, 5-04
  residuary, 5-02

divorce, 5-22, 6-03
domicile, 9-06, 11-01
due execution of will, 1-03, 2-01 *et seq.*
    attestation clause, *see* **attestation clause**
    codicil, *see* **codicils**
    date of will, 1-03
    definition of will, 2-01
    incorporation of documents, 2-12
    presumption of, 2-09
    principle of knowledge and approval, 2-10
    testator's signature, 1-03, *see also* **testator**
    witness and, *see* **witnesses**
election,
    death and non-, 5-19
    default of, 5-21
    legal right and, 5-19
    right of, 5-21
    surviving spouse, right of, 5-21
    time limit on, 5-21
equity,
    maxims,
      "equality is equity", 5-25
estate, 1-02, 5-02, *see also* **personal estate, real estate** and **residue**
    ademption, 5-04
    administration of, 1-05, 1-07, 1-08, *see* **letters of administration**
    debts payable from, 5-18
    distribution of, 1-05, 1-07
    expenses payable from, 5-18
    income of, 5-08
    interest in, 1-09
    intestate, *see* intestacy
    legal right share of spouse, *see* **legal right share of spouse**
    liabilities payable from, 5-18
    renunciation of rights to, 5-20
    sufficient assets of, 5-02
    taxation and, 5-16
    testamentary freedom to dispose of, 5-17

evidence
    affidavit, 2-10, 9-03
    copy of will as, 4-15
    death of deceased, of, 9-07, 9-13
    internal, 2-11
    last will, of, 4-12
    medical, 3-05
    nature of executor, of, 8-06
    parol, 2-12
    principle of knowledge and approval of, 2-10
    rebuttal in, 6-08
    testamentary capacity of, 3-04, 4-07, 4-09
    undue influence of, 3-06
    verify signature of deceased to, 2-09
    will made in contemplation of marriage, 4-04
executors, 7-01 *et seq, see also* **administrators**
    administration of estate by, 1-05
    appointment of, 1-02, 7-01, 7-02, 8-05, 9-01
    appropriation of deceased's estate by, 7-09
    capability of, 7-02
    citation, *see* citation
    devolution of estate to, 6-01, 7-05
    duties of, 1-02, 7-02
      assent to vesting of property, 7-08
      to administer assets, 7-06
      to distribute the estate, 7-07
      to gather assets, 7-06
    executrix, 9-05
    expressly appointed, 7-02
    functions of, 7-02
    letters of administration, *see* **letters of administration**
    liabilities of, 7-02, 7-10
    names and addresses of, 1-01, 9-05
    number of, 7-02
    oath of, 9-04, App.3, form no. 2
    powers of, 7-02
    probate, 1-05, 1-06, 1-09, *see also* **probate**

executors — *contd.*
　renunciation by, 7-03, 9-11, App 3,
　　form no.10
　son tort, 7-02
　year, of, end of, 5-09
fraud, 2-02, 3-07, 5-20, 7-02
gift, 1-02, *see* **bequest, devise, leg-
　acy, specific legacy** *and* **testa-
　mentary gifts**
　advancement and, 6-05-6-08
　codicil in, 4-18, *see also* **codicils**
　failure of, 10-02
　lapse of, 6-14
　money of, 1-02
　personal property of, 1-02
　remainder, 1-02
　residuary legatees to, 2-12
　residuary, 1-02,
　testamentary, *see* **testamentary
　　gifts**
　testator's estate, 1-02
　void, 2-08
　witness to, 2-08
grant of probate, 1-05, 1-06, 2-10,
　8-01, 8-06
　de bonis non grant, 8-05, 9-19,
　　10-06, App.3, form no. 8
　conclusive , 8-06
　citations, *see also* **citations**
　caveats, *see* **caveats**
　entitlement to apply for, 9-01
　grant in common form, 8-01
　nature of, 8-05
　necessary documentation, 9-03 *et
　　seq*
　　affidavits of due execution,
　　　9-02, 9-12
　　date of death of testator, 9-07
　　death certificate, 9-02, 9-13
　　gross value of testator's estate,
　　　9-10
　　inland revenue affidavit, 9-02,
　　　9-14-9-16
　　name and address of deceased
　　　testator, 9-06
　　name and address of executor,
　　　9-05
　　oath of executor, 9-02, 9-04

grant of probate — *contd.*
　original will and codicils, 9-02,
　　9-03,
　probate tax, 9-02, 9-17, 9-17
　relationship between executor
　　and testator, 9-08
　renunciation by executors, 9-11
　special affidavits, 9-02, 9-12
　subsequent marriage of testator,
　　9-09
　revocation of, 8-06
High Court,
　jurisdiction of, 8-01, 8-04
　President of, *see also* **intestacy**
　　corporation sole as, 6-01
　　statutory nomination of, 6-02
　　vesting of property in, 6-01,
　　　7-01
in loco parentis, 6-04, *see al*so **par-
　ents**
inheritance tax, 1-01, 5-01, 5-10 *et
　seq*
　computing tax, 5-13
　disponer, 5-11
　exemptions, 5-15
　liability to pay
　market value of property, 5-12
　preferred persons and property,
　　5-15
　successor, 5-11
interpretation of will, 5-07, *see also*
　will
intestacy, 6-01 *et seq*, 8-05
　administrators, appointment of,
　　7-04, *see* **administrators**
　advancement, *see* **advancement**
　brother's share on, 6-09
　children's share, 6-04, *see also*
　　children
　　abandonment of, 6-06
　　adopted, 6-04
　　advancement, *see* advancement
　　distribution *per stirpes* of, 6-04
　　grandchildren and, 6-04
　　illegitimate, 6-04
　　in loco parentis, 6-04,
　　legitimate, 6-04
　circumstances of, 6-01

intestacy — *contd.*
disclaiming intestate share, 6-16
expenses, payment of, 6-02
  funeral, 6-02
  testamentary, 6-02
  lawful debts, 6-02
intestate,
  definition of, 6-01
joint tenancy and, 6-03
letters of administration and, 10-7,
  11-01 *et seq*
  de bonis non grant intestate,
    11-07, App.3, form no. 9
  necessary documentation and,
    11-06
  persons entitled to apply for a
    grant, 11-01
nephew's share on, 6-10
next of kin shares on, 6-11, 6-12,
  6-13
  ascertainment of, 6-12
  search for blood relatives, 6-12
  tracing of, 6-13
niece's share on, 6-10
parent's share on, 6-08
  entitlement to, 6-08
  illegitimate children and, 6-08
partially intestate, 1-02, 5-05, 5-21,
  6-01, 6-14, App 4-04
  instances of, 6-14
President of High Court and, 6-01,
  see also **High Court**
revocation and, 4-13
rules of, 1-02, 5-05, 6-02 *et seq*
sister's share on, 6-09
state as ultimate successor, 6-15
statutory rules of, 6-01
succession rights, loss of, 6-17
surviving spouse, share of, 6-03,
  see also **legal right share of**
  spouse *and* **spouse**
  intestate share of, 6-03,
  entitlement to, 6-03
  exclusion of, 6-03
totally intestate, 5-18, 6-01

intestacy — *contd.*
wholly intestate, 11-01
will, invalidity of, 6-01, *see also*
  wills
issue, *see also* **children**
advancement and, *see* **advance-**
  ment
death of intestate with, 6-03, 6-04
death of intestate without, 6-03,
  6-11, 6-16
death without, 6-03, 6-08
equal degree of relationship of to
  deceased, 6-04
predeceased beneficiary as, 5-06
joint tenancy, 6-03
right of survivorship, 6-03
judicial separation, 6-03, 5-22
leasehold interests, 5-02
legacy, 5-01, 5-02, *see also* **bequest,**
  devise, gift, specific legacy and
  testamentary gifts
annuity, 5-02
demonstrative, 5-02
general, 5-02
pecuniary, 5-02
legal right share of spouse, 5-17 *et*
  seq, see also **spouse**
discharge of, 5-18
election, right of, 5-21
extinguishment of, 5-22
husband's, 5-19
nature of, 5-19
priority of, 5-18
renunciation of, 5-19, 5-20
right to one-half of estate, 5-18,
  5-19
right to one-third of estate, 5-18
survival of upon death, 5-19
total intestacy and, 5-18
legatee,
benefit for, 2-14
change of address of, 2-11
grant to, 10-02
residuary, 2-12, 10-02
shares given to, 5-02
sole and universal, 7-02
source of income for, 5-02

letters of administration
　alterations and, 2-10
　caveats, *see* **caveats**
　citations, *see* **citations**
　de bonis non, 1-08, 8-05, 9-19,
　　10-06, 11-07
　grant of (intestate), 11-01 *et seq*
　　de bonis non, 11-07, App.3,
　　form no.9
　necessary documentation for,
　　11-06
　persons entitled to apply for,
　　11-01-11-05
　grant of (with will), 10-01 *et seq*,
　　App.3, form no.7
　administration bond, 10-05,
　　App.3, form no.16
　administrator's oath, 10-04
　de bonis non, 10-06, App.3,
　　form no.8
　nature of, 10-01
　necessary documentation for,
　　10-03
　persons entitled to apply for,
　　10-02
　intestate, 1-07, 11-01 *et seq*, App.3,
　　form no.6, *see also* **intestacy**
　renunciation of administration,
　　App.3, form no.11
　with will annexed, App.3, form
　　no.10
　will with, 1-06
loco parentis, 6-04, 6-05, *see also*
　parents
marriage, 4-02, 4-03, 5-19, *see also*
　divorce *and* **judicial separa-
　tion**
parents,
　adopted children of, 6-08, *see also*
　　children
　illegitimate children of, 6-08, *see*
　　also **children**
　in loco parentis, 6-04, 6-05
　intestacy and, *see* intestacy
　legitimate children of, 6-08, *see*
　　also **children**
pecuniary legacy, 5-08

personal estate, 1-02, 5-02, *see also*
　bequest, estate, *and* **legacy**
　devolution of, 7-05
　jurisdiction of court and, 8-04
　personal representatives and, 7-05
　remainder of, gift of, 1-02
　residuary, gift of, 1-02, *see also*
　　residue
personal representatives, *see*
　administrators *and* **executors**
Probate, *see also* **administrators** *and*
　executors
　forms, App 3, form no.5
　grant of, *see* **grant of probate**,
　jurisdiction, 8-1 *et seq.*, *see* **pro-
　　bate jurisdiction**
　office, 1-05, 1-09, 8-02
　renunciation of (with will
　　annexed), App.3, form no.10
probate jurisdiction, 8-01 *et seq*
　contentious jurisdiction, 8-04
　　Circuit Court, 8-04
　　High Court, 8-04
　　District Probate Registry, 8-03
　non-contentious jurisdiction, 8-01
　　High Court, jurisdiction of, 8-01
　　Probate Office and, 6-02
Probate Office, 8-01, 8-02
　application for letters of adminis-
　　tration to, 8-02
　application for probate letters to,
　　8-02
Probate Officer, 8-02
　quasi-judicial powers of, 8-02
real estate, 1-02, 5-02, *see also*
　**devise, estate gift, personal
　estate** *and* **testamentary gifts**
　contents of, 7-05
　court's jurisdiction and, 8-04
　devolution of, 7-05
　meaning of, 5-02
　personal representatives and, 7-05
　remainder of, gift of, 1-02
　residuary, gift of, 1-02, *see also*
　　residue
remainder, 1-02, 4-06, 5-02, 6-03,
　7-05
reversion, 5-02, 7-05

residue, 1-02, 5-05, 10-02
    absence of gift of, 1-02
residuary clause,
    absence of, 5-21, 6-14
residuary estate of testator, 1-02,
    5-02, *see also* **testator**
residuary gift, 5-02, 5-05, 5-08
residuary legatee, 2-12, 10-02, *see*
    also **legatee**
    holding in trust, 10-02
    life interest with, 10-02
    renunciation of, 10-02
revival , 4-16 *et seq*
    codicil and, 4-16, *see also* **codicils**
    methods of, 4-16 *et seq*
    re-execution by, 4-17, *see also* **rev-**
        ocation

revocation, 1-02, 4-01 *et seq*
    capacity, 4-07, *see also* **capacity to**
        make a will
    codicil by, 4-14, *see also* **codicils**
    dependent relative, 4-15
    destruction by 4-06
    inference by, 4-08
    clause, 1-02, 6-01
    grant of representation of, 8-04
    intention of, 4-07
    intestacy, resulting in, 4-13
    methods of, 4-02 *et seq*
    presumption by, 4-09
    revival, 4-17, *see also* **revival**
    right of, 4-01
    subsequent marriage and, 4-02,
        4-03
    testamentary instrument by, 4-01,
        4-2
    will made in contemplation of mar-
        riage, 4-04
specific legacy, 5-02, 5-04, 5-08,
    7-09
solicitor,
    contractual liability, 2-14
    duty of care of, 2-14
    liability of, 2-14
    preparation of will by, 1-01, 1-03
    retention of by testator, 2-14

solicitor — *contd.*
    instructions of testator to, 1-01,
        3-04
    reading of will by, 1-03
    caveats, lodging of, 12-02, *see also*
        caveats
    evidence of, 3-05
    professional duty to draft and exe-
        cute will, 2-14
    beneficiary, duty to, 2-14
    tortious liability of, 2-14
spouse,
    intestate share of, *see* **intestacy**
    legal right share of, *see* **legal right**
        share of spouse
    provision for, 5-17
    renunciation by, App 4-06
    right to one-half of estate, 5-18
    right to one-third of estate, 5-18
state,
    bona vacantia, right of, 6-15
    escheat, right of, 6-15
    ultimate successor as, 6-15
succession
    forms
        Specimens of Assents and
            Notices, App.4, form
            no.1- App.4, form no.6
    intestate, *see* **intestacy**
survivorship,
    right of, 6-03
taxation, *see* **capital acquisitions tax**
and **inheritance tax**
Testamentary gifts, 5-01 *et seq, see*
    also **bequest, gift** *and* **legacy**
    classification of, 5-02
    failure of, 5-03 *et seq*
        beneficiary, act of and, 5-03,
            5-06
        grounds of, 5-03
        object of gift, 5-03, 5-05
        subject matter of gift and, 5-03,
            5-04
        uncertainty and, 5-07
    income from, 5-08
    inheritance tax and, *see* **inherit-**
        ance tax
    interest, accrual of on, 5-09

testator,
  beneficiaries of, 1-01, *see also*
    beneficiary
  capacity of, *see* **capacity to make
    a will**
  children of, rights of, 1-01, *see also*
    children
  death of, 2-15
  dependent children of, 1-02
  funeral expenses of, 5-17
  instructions of, 1-02
  intestate, 2-10, *see also* **intestacy**
  marital; status of, 1-02
  partially testate, 5-18, *see also*
    intestacy
  pre-existing debts of, 5-17
  signature of, 1-03, 2-02, *see also*
    due execution of will *and*
    fraud
    acknowledging of, 2-04
    codicils in, 2-13, *see also* **codi-
      cils**
    directing another to sign on
      behalf of, 2-03
    illiterate testator, 2-02, 2-10
    position of, 2-05, 2-11
    witnesses of, 2-06-2-08, *see
      also* **witnesses**
  solicitor of, *see* **solicitor**
  spouse of, rights of, 1-01, *see also*
    spouse
  testamentary expenses of, 5-17
  wholly testate, 5-18

trusts, 7-05
  administration bond and, 10-05
  devisee holding in trust, 10-02
  for sale of land, 7-05
  residuary legatee holding in trust,
    10-02

trustees, 1-02, 7-05
  for children, 1-02, 10-09, *see also*
    children
  taxable inheritance and, 5-12
undue influence, 1-04, 3-06, 3-07

will,
  alterations to, 2-10, 2-11, 9-03
  ambulatory nature of, 2-15, 4-01
  basic features of, 1-02
  capacity to make, *see* **capacity to
    make will**
  codicils to, 9-02, 9-03, *see* **codicils**
  copies of, 9-03
  construction of, *see* **construction
    of will**
  definition of, 2-01
  destruction of, 4-02, 4-05, 4-06,
    4-08, 4-15
  due execution of, *see* **due execu-
    tion of will**
  interpretation of, *see* **interpreta-
    tion of will**
  invalidity of, 1-07, 2-04, 2-11,
    2-12, 2-14, 3-01, 3-05, 3-07,
    6-01, 11-01
  memorandum to, 2-10, 2-11
  revival of, *see* revival
  revocation clause in, 1-02, *see also*
    revocation
  specimen, App. 2
  subpoena to produce, 9-03
  validity of, 1-10, 2-01
witnesses, 2-01, *see also* **evidence**
  absence of, 2-04
  attesting, 9-03
    affidavit of, 9-03, App.3, form
      no.1
  signing by, 2-06, 2-07, 2-08, 2-11,
    2-13